CROSSING JORDAN

Volume 1:
Transformational Leadership

DR. TERNAE JORDAN, SR.

Foreword By: Dr. Delatorro McNeal, II, MS, CSP, CPAE

USA Today & Wall Street Journal Best-Selling Author

Copyright © 2023 DR. TERNAE JORDAN, SR.

All rights reserved. This book or any portion thereof may not be reproduced or used in any manner whatsoever without the written consent of the author and copyright holder. Brief excerpts for use of quotations in a book review must give proper citing to the author. For information regarding bulk purchases of this book, digital purchases, and special discounts, please contact the author.

First printing, 2023. United States of America.

ISBN: 979-8-9889314-0-9

DEDICATION

It is with great pleasure that I dedicate this book to my father, the late Dr. Melvin Jordan, the man who gave me vision and taught me what a Godly man looks like; one who walked with godly principles. Though not perfect, he was indeed a man after God's own heart. Dad, it is because of you that I have been inspired to write this Crossing Jordan book. You provided a rock-solid foundation for your family. Your faith in God was contagious, and we now enjoy the fruits and heritage of your labor. Thank you for being such an awesome example for your family.

It was very painful to watch you cross your Jordan the final time, however, we rejoice, knowing we will see you someday in the promised land.

Love your son,
Dr. Ternae T. Jordan, Sr.

Table of Contents

	Acknowledgments	i
	Foreword	vii
	Introduction	Pg 1
1	Born in the Jordan	Pg 7
2	Growing Up Jordan	Pg 21
3	Coming of Age	Pg 29
4	The Middle Passage	Pg 41
5	The Next Passage	Pg 51
6	The Return to Egypt	Pg 73
7	The Love of My Life	Pg 79
8	Call into Ministry: The Story	Pg 103
	About the Author	Pg 129

Acknowledgments

Before I even thought to set pen to paper, God blessed me by placing so many amazing people in my life who would prepare me for the task of writing this book. I could easily fill multiple pages with the names of friends and family members who have somehow influenced me along my journey, however, I especially want to thank the following individuals:

My father, Dr. Melvin Jordan, was a powerful man of God whom I loved dearly. I dedicate this book to you, Dad.
My mother, Maggie Jordan, who gave me life, loved, and cared for me unconditionally; one who was always my greatest encourager and supporter. Mama, you gave me my passion for God and love for His people. I will love you always.

I'm grateful for the blessing of my brother and sisters - Gail, Michael, and Kimberly. You guys have brought so much spice into my life. No human could ask for better siblings. I love you guys to the moon and back. Thanks for loving and always supporting my visions.

My beautiful wife, Angela Faye, I thank God for placing you as my guardian angel for over 55 years ago. You have walked with me through the good and the bad, the mountain tops, and the valleys. We have crossed the

Jordan on so many levels together. You motivated me with your love and support from a boy to a man, to a father and a pastor. You blessed me with three exceptional children who, because of your amazing example, all walk with God. You are indeed the wind beneath my wings. Thank you for your undying love, support, and encouragement. I love you forever, and I shall forever be indebted to you my love.

To my two sons, Ternae and Jamichael, the two men that I admire and look up to. I'm very proud of the men you have become; men who have tremendous vision at such young ages. The Jordan legacy is truly in good hands for generations because of the vision and passion you both possess. You are both amazing men of God. Continue to walk in His ways, as He continues to lift you higher, and your dreams become your reality.

To my daughter, Dejuan, you are indeed the apple of my eye. Thank you for catching your daddy's vision of stopping the madness. Your passion for others and your commitment to the mission of impacting lives is unlimited. Thank you for being a woman of excellence and continue to soar. Daddy loves you madly.

To my daughters-in-law, Demetria, and Amanda, two incredible women that God added to my life. I'm grateful for you both and the gift of love that you bring to my world.

Last, but certainly not least, this crossing Jordan legacy shall be passed on to my four grandchildren Deanna, Micah, Nason, and Asa. You guys are the love and reflection of G-Poppie's life that will carry on our Jordan Legacy. Remember to always keep God first and He will add all other things that your heart desires. G-Poppie loves you guys forever. Keep crossing your Jordans and make the world a better place.

Mrs. Rosetta Russell has served as my family's guardian angel for over 23 years. Rosetta, your commitment and unwavering love for us shall never be forgotten. Your protection and covering shall always be remembered and we shall always be indebted to you. Thank you for all you mean to us.

I also honor a great and impactful personal mentor by the name of Dr. Riggins R. Earl, Jr. He walked into my life in 1973 in a religious studies classroom at the University of Tennessee Knoxville. He challenged my perspective, opened my eyes to the social justice aspect of the gospel message, and broadened my vision. My perception and passion to impact lives through the Gospel has shifted and matured because of him. I will forever be indebted to you, Dr. Riggins, for your impartation.

There is no way that I can leave out a spiritual son turned mentor, Dr. Delatorro McNeal, II. You have been such a thriving force who has stretched me and allowed me to see the vast role I have access to in the marketplace. Thank you for believing in me, but also holding me accountable to the vision and helping me connect the dots. I appreciate who you are and how you continue to set me up for success.

To my publisher, Ebony Walker, I extend my heartfelt

thanks for the tireless effort you put into making this book the best it can be. Thank you for your unwavering support, patience, and genuine enthusiasm to make this collaboration a memorable and rewarding journey. Your ability to strike the perfect balance between professional expertise and personal camaraderie has made all the difference.

Finally, to my editor, Beverly Sonnier, your keen editorial eye and insightful suggestions have breathed life into my words. Your ability to see the heart of my story, to understand its essence, and to help me shape it into something even more beautiful has been nothing short of miraculous.

CROSSING JORDAN

DR. TERNAE JORDAN, SR.

CROSSING JORDAN

*Volume 1:
Transformational Leadership*

DR. TERNAE JORDAN, SR.

Foreword By: Dr. Delatorro McNeal, II, MS, CSP, CPAE

USA Today & Wall Street Journal Best-Selling Author

Foreword

In the vast tapestry of life, our beginnings often hold the seeds of profound transformation and wisdom. We can't look at where we are now, nor where we are headed, without looking at who and what we've come from. As it pertains to building the internal fortitude of an authentic leader, that is the essence of what "Crossing Jordan" offers us.

As human beings, we are intricately shaped by our experiences, and the journey of crossing from one phase of life to another - akin to crossing the river Jordan - symbolizes the transitions that define us. In this eloquent work, Dr. Ternae Jordan, Sr. embarks on a poignant exploration of the impact that his origins have had on his leadership capabilities within a variety of arenas.

As leaders, whether in our personal lives or professional domains, the wisdom found in these pages encourages us to reclaim and honor our past to foster a profound sense of self-awareness. This self-awareness causes us to hold onto the lessons of old, no matter how we received them or who we received them from, while respecting and holding dear the intricate lessons learned throughout.

"Crossing Jordan" illustrates the vital truth that the teachings imprinted in our beginnings act as foundational stones throughout our life and leadership endeavors. By understanding the intricate threads of our personal narratives, we gain the invaluable gift of empathy and relatability - two extremely quintessential traits of impactful leadership.

As we embark on the first volume of this enlightening trilogy, I encourage you, the reader, to immerse yourself in the rich tapestry of "Crossing Jordan." Embrace the invitation to envelop your own story, for therein lies the gateway to transcendent leadership - one that is anchored in integrity, affinity, and an unyielding commitment to growth.

Prepare to be moved, challenged, and transformed as you choose to intentionally journey through "Crossing Jordan."

-Dr. Delatorro McNeal, II, MS, CSP, CPAE
Hall of Fame Keynote Speaker & Peak Performance Expert
USA Today and Wall Street Journal Best Selling Author
"Shift Into a Higher Gear: Better Your Best and Live Life to the Fullest"

CROSSING JORDAN

Introduction

What do you think of when you think of the Jordan River? To me, the Jordan River is probably one of the most symbolic rivers and bodies of water in the world. It has its significance in both the Old and New Testaments. And while it may not be the deepest river, it is yet one of the dirtiest rivers. Also, it runs 156 miles from north to south, feeding into the Seas of Galilee and ending in the Dead Sea.

As a man of faith, the Jordan River symbolizes moving from the wilderness to the Promised Land. It is the place where the leadership mantle shifted from Moses to Joshua, as the children of Israel passed over into the land that God promised Abraham, who was also called the "Father of Faith." It also represents a place of transition, for it was at the Jordan where Elijah transferred his prophetic mantle to his mentee, Elisha, just before he boarded the fiery chariot and ascended into heaven. It was at Jordan where John the Baptist baptized his cousin, Jesus. This act would propel him into His earthly ministry.

Christians have often used the symbol of the Jordan River as the saints passing from earthly life to eternal life. In other words, the term "Crossing Jordan" symbolizes crossing into a better place and describes the place where one receives his heavenly reward for living a fruitful and effective life. In my personal journey, the Jordan River becomes a metaphorical symbol for transitioning from one season of my life to the next.

As a man of professionalism, I have adapted to the viewpoint of "Crossing Jordan" being a metaphorical expression, describing the process of venturing out. In one's career or professional development, it becomes mandatory for one to step outside of their comfort zone and take a leap of faith. That is the only way to explore new opportunities and conquer challenges. When you embrace your Jordan, in whatever sense, you embrace change and adaptability. You embrace the lessons that come with every part of that process. You embrace the unknown, believing that it will create something greater and grander.

Adaptability is a highly sought-after competency in today's workplace and corporate fields, as well as any location where leadership is necessary. Professionals who demonstrate their ability to cross Jordan by adapting to new circumstances display their resilience and capacity to thrive in challenging environments. They also show that they have an innate desire to pursue growth and attain it. Successful professionals recognize that growth occurs outside their comfort zones. Crossing Jordan is an essential step in the journey of continuous improvement, where individuals push their boundaries and actively seek challenges that stretch their capabilities."

The name "Jordan" is unique, having both Greek and Hebrew origins. It can be traced to the popular river in Israel. In Hebrew, the name means to "flow down" or to "descend" into the deep. Throughout my life I have tried to honor and protect the Jordan name. I remember as a child my father, who has always been my hero, saying to me, *"Ternae, I may not be able to leave you great riches, houses, or land; but the one thing I can give you is a good name."* He taught me to always protect the name because a good name will open doors that no man can close and get you into places where your money cannot.

That statement holds true, as I have carefully protected and honored my name, allowing it to make room for me. You see, your name is a gift. And when you have gifts, they always open doors for you. They always allow others to see what they need that's inside of you. And I, for one, am grateful for having a name that precedes me.

The purpose of this book is to honor the name and legacy of the man who deposited so much into my life. The knowledge, wisdom, and spirituality that flowed down from my "Jordan" has given me the strength to descend deep and to transition from one season of life to the next. I pray that this book serves as a roadmap of sorts for you. There is a level of personal and professional development that will come through the wisdom shared within. It is my story of the seasons, transitions, and journey of faith that was downloaded into me from this great man named "Jordan." As we pass through Jordan together, I pray that you will gather stones of faith, integrity, forgiveness, commitment, love, desire, creativity, and mentorship. With these stones, once you reach the other side, you will also leave a legacy that will live on forever and impact nations from the inside out.

As we embark on this book, I encourage you to perceive it beyond a mere personal narrative. Delve into its depths and unravel the hidden messages that openly portray the essence of triumph and leadership. Seek connections with relatable life circumstances that can serve as stepping stones for personal and professional growth. It matters not who you are, where you are from, or how you appear; each of us possesses a unique story that offers fragments of evidence. These fragments hold the potential for progress, internal development, and expansion. All that is required is an open mind and a willingness to venture across uncharted territory. The unfolding wonders on the other side remain unknown until you take that leap.

CROSSING JORDAN

DR. TERNAE JORDAN, SR.

CHAPTER 1

Born in the Jordan

I sat by his bedside as he grasped for breath. I knew that the day had finally come. It was exceedingly difficult to watch, and I struggled to wrap my mind around it. The man who had given me life, the one who taught me everything I knew, the one who had been a powerful influence in my life, was finally taking his final breath. I had heard him cry out many times, *"Lord, please come, take me."* I held back my emotions knowing that this awesome father, grandfather, mentor, visionary, patriot, pastor, influencer, and leader was now crossing Jordan. As my mother, my three siblings, his grandchildren, and close family members stood around his bedside, it was difficult to watch him gasping for breath. He had lived a good fruitful life. I could not understand how after all he had done as a faithful soldier for the Lord and how he served others, why a faithful God would allow him to suffer and struggle with his crossing Jordan transition. No matter how hard this moment was, I knew he was leaving a great legacy behind and passing the baton to his children and grandchildren to run the next leg of life's relay.

Melvin Jordan was born to Green and Mahalia Jordan in Limestone County Alabama on September 24, 1931. He was the oldest of 10 children and spent much of his early years raising his younger siblings. Melvin's father was a sharecropper. Melvin, with his other brothers and sisters, worked alongside their parents in the cotton fields. He attended Walters Chapel Church School while laboring in the cotton fields to help support his family.

Maggie Brown, my mother, was also born in Madison County, Alabama to William and Jessie Brown. She was the second oldest of 10 children and likewise, spent her early years working in the cotton fields on the land of her family's landowner, Mr. Jody Pettit. She attended the Capshaw School that was also run by the church, as most Negro schools were in those days.

Maggie met Melvin in September of 1949 at Saint James Hall Church. He was one of the lead singers in a gospel quartet called the Silver Trumpets. His father, Green, served as their manager. They traveled throughout the church circuit in northern Alabama with their special brand of gospel singing that brought down the house everywhere they went.

Melvin was the lead singer on the song entitled, "What a Time, What a Time, Great God Almighty, What a Time." In Maggie's own words, *"He really could sing that song. We followed them around and when they sang on the radio, people would always request Melvin's song. He really was a very spiritual and handsome young man. What really attracted me to him was that he was so nice and humble. His personality really was such that people were drawn to him."* Melvin, however, remembered things quite differently. He said, *"I remember Maggie as a great dancer. I loved watching her at a gathering spot called The Log Cabin. I could not dance, but it was worth the trip to watch Maggie cut a rug on that dance floor."*

Melvin and Maggie only dated for six months. On February 26th, 1950, at the age of 18 and 19, they were married in a quiet ceremony by Reverend Jackson on the front porch of the Brown's family shack. That night, they returned to Melvin's apartment in Decatur, Alabama. The couple lived in Decatur from February until September of 1950, at which time Melvin moved to Chattanooga, Tennessee to look for employment. He moved in with Maggie's aunt and uncle, Louise and Jimmy Lee Ford. Melvin quickly secured a job at Southern Allied Foundry, and within three weeks returned to Madison County to retrieve his bride. On their return to Chattanooga, they moved into a boarding house on Market Street owned by Miss Katie Cotton. There, they rented a bedroom and shared the kitchen with other tenants.

On July 14, 1952, Melvin was drafted into the United States Army and was shipped off to fight in the Korean War for the next two years. Maggie returned to her parents' home to wait for her husband's return. On April 13, 1954, Melvin was honorably discharged and reunited with his wife. They moved back to Chattanooga, and he went to work at the Wheland Foundry, pouring iron. Melvin wanted his own place so badly that he took on a second job at Crane Foundry. They were soon able to rent an apartment on 24th Street and there they set up housekeeping for the next few years.

Melvin was always a hard worker. For over 20 years, he worked hard labor to support his family. Sometimes he would work two or three jobs at once while also driving a taxicab at night. In 1961, Melvin felt the overwhelming pressure to heed the call to preach the gospel of Jesus Christ. Maggie was traumatized. She had always said she would never be married to a preacher because of the amount of time they must spend away from their family. After much prayer, God gave her the peace and assurance that if He called him, He would also provide. So, with her blessings, Melvin preached his initial sermon and was licensed to preach the gospel in November 1961. Eight months later, in 1962, he was called to pastor Mount Canaan Baptist Church where he served faithfully for the next 40 years.

Now, allow me to put a pin right here. You might be reading this and wondering what in the world this has to do with anything. You may even be considering how this information benefits you. Well, remember how we briefly mentioned the "stones" in our introduction? That's right, these are all a part of identifying those stones. While this portion of the story might seem insignificant, it lays the foundation for what a leader looks like. It is highlighting something that we'll discuss more in this book: *sacrifice.* In order to get to a place of success and settlement, there were many transitions that took place. Much compromise took place. A great deal of sacrifice was necessary. And in Melvin's own way, from serving the military to working multiple jobs, he was exemplifying the characteristics of proper leadership. Only through those lessons could he embark upon this next phase, this next transition of life. Now let's dig a little deeper into what happens next.

For years, Melvin and Maggie prayed for a child. Maggie had gone back and forth to the doctor to see why they could not conceive. I remember them sharing the story of how they prayed night and day to have a child. They, like Hannah, the mother of Samuel in the Bible, promised God that if He would bless them to conceive a son, they would dedicate that son back to God. In March of 1955, Maggie went to visit her doctor, Dr. Binder. It was he who informed her that she was pregnant. In case you haven't caught on, it was me that she and my father conceived. In sharing the story with me, she mentioned that she and Dad were the happiest people in the world. They lived with anticipation of the day that their firstborn child would enter the world. On a very cold morning of December 3, 1955, in Carver Hospital, another level of legacy and leadership was born; and that legacy began with me. Ironically, this also happened to be the same year that Emmitt Till was lynched and murdered in Mississippi. In essence, as someone who could have been a world changer, but was taken unnecessarily from this earth, another one was presented.

Here's a bit of history about Carver Memorial Hospital. It was a hospital for Negroes, named after the African American agricultural scientist and inventor, George Washington Carver. It opened on June 18, 1947, and was formerly the old West Ellis Hospital. This healthcare facility was said to have been the first municipal-owned and tax-supported hospital in America. Also, it was staffed entirely by all Negro doctors, nurses, and other personnel for the care of Negro patients. Carver hospital closed in 1962.

On the day I was born, Dad was running late to the hospital. Mom told me that she was so excited to name me that she could not wait until Dad arrived.. The name of the French doctor who delivered me was Dr. Ternae Tsargaris. Mom told me she loved how unique and different that name was and believed that I would be a special and blessed child. Therefore, by the time Dad arrived at the hospital, she had already placed my name on the birth certificate. She named me after the doctor who delivered me. I entered the world as Ternae Tsargaris Jordan. On that day I was born into the "Jordan" as an added piece of a great family lineage; one that I was destined to continue and make even greater.

Consider that for a moment, even with your personal life and story of your existence. Do you believe that you were added to a legacy to enhance that legacy? Do you recognize that there is a missing puzzle piece, a missing link, that only you can fill? Most times, we don't pay attention to what's in and on our family, so we miss out on what we are created to add to it. Regardless of the dynamics of one's bloodline, each person plays a vital role in adding value to that bloodline. Therefore, leadership and legacy were already in you before you even knew who and what you were.

I often desired to know the meaning of the name "*Ternae.*" In my effort to research it, I found several descriptive statements connected that describe me adequately:

1. You like to control everyone within your influence to shape things to your own liking.

2. If positive, you develop high spirituality, as you have God's protection.

3. You are sensitive, affectionate, imaginative, cooperative, spiritually aware, and prone to self-sacrifice.

4. You can keep secrets and are a good diplomat.

5. You have an eventful exciting life.

6. You are versatile and can learn easily.

7. You desire to inspire and lead to control other affairs.

8. You are courteous and bold, action oriented, energetic, and strong-willed.

9. You want to make a difference in the world, and this attitude often attracts you to cultural interest, politics, social issues, and the cultivation of your creative talents.

These characteristics describe me well. The part that truly has been a major element of my journey in life is the fact that I've always felt and believed that I had God's special protection. It is because of this story of my birth that I have always felt a close, spiritual connection to God.

Have you looked into the story of your birth? As a great asset to society and a powerful leader (because that is who and what you are), it is nice to have these tidbits of information. No, your story does not have to be like mine or that of anyone else's. The important part, however, is that you're here and you're full of value and purpose. Whether you research your name, your lineage, or even the story of your arrival, every portion of your life – great, not so great, and in between – make up the greatest gift to the world, which is you. As you grow into a shifter, a transformational leader, and one who does much with little, you'll begin to see just how necessary your wisdom and expertise really are.

In 1957, my sister Gail was born. She and I became good friends and confidants. I absolutely love my sister. She is a person with a big heart and will do anything within her power to help or impact someone else's life. Gail and I became good buddies and got in too much trouble together. I will always remember the day we were playing in my mother and father's closet looking for my father's boots so that we could play like firemen. I lit a match and as the match burned down, it also burned my finger. And when I dropped it on the laundry paper, it caught my dad's clothes and suits on fire. Mama was on the phone and rather than disturb her I grabbed Gail by the hand, and we quietly went and sat on the couch while smoke began to fill the house. The firemen were called, they came and put the fire out easing the neighborhood panic. That evening when Dad came home, he set us both on the couch to determine who set the closet on fire. To this day I owe my loving sister Gail an apology because I sat back and allowed her to take the blame for something that I had done. That's another reason why I love my sister so much. She has always cared for and protected me. I owe her a great debt for always being my source of support. Even without my recognizing it then, my sister was the epitome of leadership. Sometimes, you have to be willing to take one for the team. It can't always be about proving that you are innocent, as much as it might be proving that you can take the blows. No, it may not always be fair; it does, however, work something much greater within you that makes you trustworthy and dependable. That's leadership in and of itself.

In addition to being blessed with wonderful parents and a loving sister, our family added a new edition with the birth of my younger brother, Michael Jordan in 1960. There was an actor on the set of one of the daytime soaps named Michael Anthony. My mother loved his name so much that she named my baby brother Michael Anthony Jordan. I vaguely remember the day that we brought this new baby boy home. I remember being amazed at this new life being brought into the world and being added to our family. Michael was an intuitive baby; incredibly quiet and laid-back, different from the noisy, loud babies that we had seen on TV. Our family was now growing and expanding. Now added to the Jordan clan of Melvin, Maggie, Gail and Ternae, was this amazing new bundle of joy.

My youngest sister, Kimberly Denise Jordan, was born March 28, 1970. I was a sophomore in high school and was totally surprised when my mother, who was approximately 40 years old at this time, informed us that our family was growing. I was already moving through high school and the next phase of my Jordan journey. However, I was overjoyed to know that – at such a late age – my mother was giving birth and adding to our legacy. Kim came into our lives at a time when I was preparing to move out of the home. In her early years, I have very little remembrance of her. However, I do recall when I first laid eyes on her. She stole my heart and I've never been prouder of or adored anyone more than I did my baby sister. She was a breath of fresh air. Kim would later grow up to possess one of the greatest singing voices that I have ever heard. I would strongly compare her gift to that of the late great Aretha Franklin. She sang with so much heart and so much soul that it would change atmospheres as soon as the microphone was in her hands. If you ever heard her, you would never be the same. I do know that she also stole my father's and mother's heart. I watched her get away with things that never would have been allowed amongst my other two siblings or myself.

As a child I often followed my father around from church to church and place to place as he delivered the Word of God and cared for the members of his church family. I've always enjoyed hearing good preaching and singing and could sing a little bit myself. But even at this age, I didn't know that I was following leadership. I longed to be in the presence of power, of strength, and of those who could carry weights, seemingly effortless.

My first real encounter with the presence of God was at the age of 6 years old during a revival service at the Mount

Canaan Baptist Church where dad pastored. It was an old-fashioned revival service where a well-known powerful black preacher named Amos Donaldson from northern Alabama was preaching a 5-night revival. Mount Canaan was a small reddish color shack-like building in a run-down neighborhood called "The Bucket of Blood." It was called the bucket of blood because every Friday and Saturday night there would be house parties, and oftentimes fights would break out where it was said that blood would run down those streets.

The church had a cast iron pot-belly stove in the center to keep us warm on cold winter days as we worshiped God. On this particular night, the spirit of God was high in the place, the choir was singing and there was foot-stomping that always brings back memories of what the old black Baptist church was like. That night as Pastor Donaldson was preaching, there was an awesome presence in the air and atmosphere; one filled with jubilance, joy, and praise. The energy was high in that room. As I sat there on the front row on that hard mahogany bench known as "the mourners' bench," I felt an emotion that I had never experienced before.

Growing up in the black Baptist church, I had always heard of the spirit of God, but on that night something came over me and when I came to myself, I was sitting in the chair that was placed in the middle of the room for those who came off of the mourners' bench. I was rejoicing and declaring that I had accepted Jesus as my personal Savior and wanted Him to be guardian and Lord of my life. From that moment on, I've always felt a special connection and relationship with God and have known that He had something special for me to do. I've always loved and cared for people and have a servant's heart, but I knew there was more. Even though I was very young, there was this urge in me to help others. Mom and dad were very excited about the decision that I had made. From that time on, I began to sing in various places where my dad went to preach. When I would sing it would often move people, as the old folks would say it made them "catch the spirit."

I really loved to sing. In fact, in my early years I sang with a group of young men that I grew up with in Mount Canaan. We were named the Gospel Sevettes. We connected at church and were organized under the leadership of Mrs. Esther Smith, a great gospel singer in her own right. She later became Mrs. Esther Graham after she married a deacon of the church. Our singing group consisted of Leroy (McClure) Cooper and his twin brother, Leon (McClure) Cooper, Curtis Walker, LeBron Hicks, Thomas Reid Jr., Michael Green, my little brother, Michael Jordan, and myself.

Pastor Melvin Jordan was called to pastor the Mount Canaan Baptist Church on the fourth Sunday in August 1962, eight months after he preached his introduction sermon. The church membership consisted of approximately 15 members who were currently without a leader. Melvin Jordan began to preach the gospel and many people were added to that number. Then, there became an urgent need for a larger sanctuary. It was a challenge and a great struggle getting the members to accept the pastor's vision for the new building and its relocation to a different site.

Chapter 1 Building Blocks

1. How you *start* holds more weight than you can imagine. Looking into the beginning always allows you to see the direction of the compass.

2. Choosing to push through adversity has benefits. Every situation might not be the *ideal* situation, but you have the power to use it as fuel for the journey.

3. Your role in your family unit is about more than just being a child, sibling, parent, etc. Recognize that you were made to enhance your legacy.

4. Who you follow sets you up for who will follow you one day. Pay attention to who and what you gravitate towards.

DR. TERNAE JORDAN, SR.

CHAPTER 2

Growing Up Jordan

Growing up, my family lived in a tight closed-in apartment at 613 North Holly Street, Apartment A. At five years old, I was ready to face the world and excited to meet my kindergarten teacher, Ms. Broadway, a tall, respected, dark-skinned woman who became the early learning teacher for all the neighborhood kids. Her kindergarten classes were taught in the same house that she lived in which was located a few doors up from our apartment. Ms. Broadway loved kids and was excited to prepare us to face a world of segregation and racism, believing that an education would be the doorway to a brighter future for children of color.

I remember my mother dressing me in white knee length pants with a white shirt and white shoes for the first day of school. That morning, she took me by the hand and walked me proudly towards the yellow and white house with bright colored flowers and colorful animals painted on it. The bright colors also complemented Ms. Broadway's personality. She was a very pleasant, yet stern woman with an engaging personality.

Growing up in the Churchville community of Chattanooga was very exciting. We were poor but didn't even know it. We were surrounded by good neighbors who, like everyone else, were struggling to raise their children in an uncomfortable and racist environment. Most of our neighbors were church people who were trying to live by the Golden Rule, *"Do unto others as you would have them do unto you."* We were surrounded by good people like Mr. L.B and his wife Betty Hayes who lived in Apartment B directly behind our small apartment. Across the street was Mr. Joe and Alberta Cunningham, and the Tolliver family lived next door. Mr. Dan and Symlu Tolliver had 5 girls: Iciephine, Maggie, Danyetta, Joyce, and Janice. This family treated me and my sister Gail, who was two years younger than I, like part of their family. And since there were no boys in their family, Iciephine, the oldest of the girls, became my personal caretaker and defender. She was 11 years older than me and a self-proclaimed tomboy. She took me under her wings to help me transition into adolescence.

When my mom took her first job, Iciephine was there to look after Gail and me. I remember the first fight I got into with a neighborhood kid. I was a very sensitive child who did not like trouble or confrontation. As a matter of fact, I've always been sort of an emotional crybaby. On one particular day, while playing in the street with the other kids, one boy pushed me down, causing me to scrape my knee. I went running and crying, almost traumatized by the confrontation. To whom did I run? Yes, my protector and hero, Iciephine who immediately scolded and told me that I must learn to take care of myself or else end up always being pushed around or taken advantage of. She then put her fist up and showed me how to protect myself. Once the lesson was over, she sent me back to the street to confront the boy who pushed me down. As I walked up to him with my fists clenched and my eyes closed, I reared back and proceeded to punch him in the nose. When I opened my eyes, I saw blood running from this kid's nose and Iciephine standing by, encouraging, and cheering me on. After that day, none of the neighborhood kids ever bothered me again.

My mom, whom I loved, always treated me with great respect and adoration. She taught me to respect others and to always carry myself in a positive and respectful way. Mom, who was a very caring, but stern woman, treated me not only as her son, but also as a brother in many instances. She respected my wisdom even at a young age and often asked my opinion on many issues that she confronted.

I have always been a Bible student. After accepting Jesus into my life at the age of six years old, I became fascinated with the Bible. On many Saturday evenings my dad would ask me to go out and gather all the neighborhood kids for a Saturday evening Bible study. I could not wait to gather them in our tiny apartment where Dad would ask us questions about the Bible. I was always jumping up, raising my hand trying to answer the questions and impress him before any other kid had a chance to do so. This would become very frustrating to Dad, and he would try to keep me from taking over the class by saying, *"Ternae, give the other kids a chance to respond."*

I wanted to show what I knew, and even show that I had leadership qualities. I was willing to take the initiative and speak up when others did not. However, the correction from my father showed me another side to real leadership. You have to be willing to give people a chance. While you may know "how" to do a thing, it might not be your season *to* do that thing. And believe me, I knew the answers. But silence can be golden and can help others to find their voice.

After a visit to a Bible camp called Camp Cedine in Spring City, Tennessee, I started receiving weekly Bible studies from The Mailbox Club to fill out and return. I would wait patiently by the mailbox each week to receive my Bible study. Then, I would quickly open it, quickly respond to all the questions, and quickly send it back. One of my greatest joys was waiting each week for my new lesson and the return of my previous one which always received a gold star and a beautiful red special honors tag. I credit this activity as creating in me "a true love for God's Word" that continues to be a big part of my life even unto this day.

I was always a lover of kids and always had a caring heart for others in the community. So, everywhere Iciephine went, I would always want to tag along behind her and to my delight, she always let me. She was my best friend.

Let's reflect on a thought-provoking question: Who is

willing to be led by you? It may have initially seemed that this was merely a story about a young boy drawn to someone adventurous. However, my friend possessed distinct attributes and leadership qualities that instilled in me a sense of trust, allowing her to take the lead. Whether you hold the position of a CEO, supervisor, shift manager, teacher, or the head of your family, what is it about you that inspires others to follow? I encourage you to conduct a self-analysis, recognizing and emphasizing those qualities within you that pave the way for others to tread upon.

There weren't a lot of things for African American kids to do while I was growing up, but one of the things we truly looked forward to was walking over to Lincoln Park. It was the only public park in the city where people of color could go to have fun, but to get there, we had to walk past Warner Park, which was reserved for Whites only, then walk across the viaduct, over the train tracks, and pass a neighborhood where a gang would terrorize us. However, it was all worth it because we were so proud of our Lincoln Park.

The Lincoln Park area was a place where many of Chattanooga's celebrities grew up and around there; people like the movie actor Samuel Jackson, singers Usher Raymond, Fred Cash, Sam Gooden, and Richard, Arthur and Brooks who later hooked up with two famous guys out of Chicago, Curtis Mayfield and Jerry Butler to form the world-renowned R&B group, "The Impressions." No matter the challenges we experienced to get there, we would not allow anything to deprive us of our time of freedom to just be kids in Lincoln Park.

Once we got there, Iciephine would take me by the hand and lead me over to this beautiful haven with a musical carousel, ferris wheel, swings, sliding boards, see-saws, an arcade game room and cages full of monkeys that we loved to watch and feed. It was a place of pride and history for our Black community, and it was always a joy to go there.

There was also a huge swimming pool in the park, but I was not a swimmer and was really afraid of the water. Emmitt Till had been murdered in 1955, the same year I was born. His story and other gory stories I'd heard growing up containing details about young African Americans drowning, being lynched, and thrown into rivers had a chilling effect on me and my lack of desire to learn how to swim. However, later in life I developed a true love for water. Even now, when I want to find my place of peace, I go down to the Tennessee River, or cross the Caribbean Sea on a cruise ship, or take a flight to Jamaica just to lay around the beautiful blue waters of the Caribbean because it provides so much peace and tranquility for my soul.

What is your sanctuary? Where do you cultivate tranquility and foster personal growth? This scenario presents a compelling illustration of the principles of self-care and deliberate development. Once you choose to liberate yourself from the constraints of fear, that which you previously dismissed can transform into a sanctuary of solace. Every leader necessitates a designated retreat, a place of respite. Whether it manifests as a waterfront vista, a mountainous refuge, or an urban landscape ablaze with vibrant lights, ensure that you purposefully invest in rejuvenating your inner being.

Chapter 2 Building Blocks

1. Learn to share the spotlight. A good leader may always have the answers, but a mature leader allows others to exercise their mental fortitude.

2. Self-care is not a cute catchphrase; it's a way of life. Be intentional about finding your place of solace and tranquility.

3. Once you have mastered locating your peaceful place, encourage those who "follow" you to do the same. It's one thing to take advantage of self-care moments, but make sure that those who trust you know that the same is acceptable for them.

DR. TERNAE JORDAN, SR.

CHAPTER 3

Coming of Age

In the fall of 1961, I started first grade at Orchard Knob Elementary School. It was located on an historic hill where the Civil War had been fought. How ironic for a school for African American kids to be built on a hill where blood had been shed a hundred years earlier to keep our ancestors in slavery!

You may not see the irony in that but allow me to explain. Imagine a place being laced with dread, but later being a foundation for destiny. Picture the most horrific aftermath of bodies and blood, atop a hill, which would someday free the very ones it tried to encapsulate. In my humble opinion, this fact alone proves that greatness can come from something gory. It sheds light on how some of the bravest and boldest human beings can be planted in horrific soil and still grow beautifully. Isn't that just like leadership?

How many times, as a leader or the head of anything, have you had to come into a horrible situation and make it something productive? Have you ever been led to a place of destitution and been entrusted with remodeling the outcome of it? I know we're talking about land and school but it's more to it than that. The fact that this school was built on a hill in a place of death shows that the right person and the right location can bring about the right change. Along with that is the value of education.

We were always told that education was the way for advancement, especially if you wanted to grow and prosper. I remember walking into the dark halls of that run down building, holding tightly to my mother's hand as she passed me off to a stranger named Mrs. Julia Pettijohn, a beautiful young woman about my mother's age. Mrs. Pettijohn was a pleasant and approachable woman. I still remember that day when Mom transferred my hand to Mrs. Pettijohn's hand, and I began the adventure of preparing myself for the future. Again, we have another lesson to highlight.

Whether you are leading in the marketplace, at home, or any structured organization, can your hands be trusted? Are you able to help walk someone towards the next portion of their destiny? And are you trusted to guide them to the help they need? As a leader, our hands are vital because we want to ensure that they can be trusted to guide without evil intent.

Orchard Knob was the neighborhood school. That meant every kid in our neighborhood also attended the school. Mrs. Pettijohn gave me my thirst for wisdom and knowledge. I shall ever be grateful to her. She believed in me, and it became evident so much that I quickly became the "teacher's pet." She also became a person that I would know and respect for the rest of my life. As I grew older, we would often cross paths as we maneuvered in African American church circles. I would go to her church, and she spent a lot of time at mine. I remember her being so proud of my growth and my ability to articulate the Word of God. It was always a delight that the woman who grabbed my hand as a young lad saw me grab the hand of many others and lead them.

I attended Orchard Knob Elementary for first through third grades. I was also blessed to have Mrs. Harris as my second-grade teacher. Like Mrs. Pettijohn, she also truly believed in me and poured into me, both educationally and spiritually. She was a pastor's wife and understood my zest for God and the call that was on my life even at such a young age. I tell you, it's vital that others can see what's in you and on you – even when you don't fully understand it.

In the spring of 1963, my father came home and told my mother that he was buying us a new house. It was located at 1316 Wheeler Avenue in the Avondale Community. Avondale was a former all white community that quickly became filled with Black families, after what was known as the "White Flight." I remember my dad coming in and saying to me, *"Ternae you have the option of continuing at your present school, but you are zoned to attend Avondale Elementary School and this school will be an integrated one."* Being a young, bright eyed adventurous kid, I always wanted to try new things, so I told my dad I wanted to go to the new school. In 1963 there was a lot of discussion, dialogue, and feuding about allowing black kids to integrate with white kids. It was in this community that I experienced my next Crossing Jordan "place of transition," growing from my early childhood years to my adolescence and later teenage years.

We moved into the Avondale Community and, like most communities in those days, whites started moving out when black people started moving in. Many other families of color were moving in at the same time we were and there were many children on our street who were my age. I was able to develop a whole new set of friends. The families on our street became "our family." In those days, we truly had a real neighborhood. Today, the word *neighbor* has been removed from the community and now they are simply called "hoods." The adults who lived on our street could reprimand and chastise every child on the block and then call our parents; by the time we arrived home, we would be reprimanded again. Oh, how I miss those days when children were respectful of adults and adults were tremendous examples for kids.

Some of the families who lived on our street included: Taylors, Whites, Walkers, Toneys, Overtons, Colemans, Lindseys, and the Players. I developed many friends in this community. We did many things that kids did, like playing hide and seek, and our version of street football.

The Pattons lived behind our house. Their father was also a pastor. They had a number of children and older male relatives. That's how I learned to play football, basketball, and baseball along with the other young boys in our tight-knit community.

My best friend was Curtis Walker. The Walker family also attended our church. His father, Mr. Walter Lee Walker, was a deacon at the church and his mother, Buel Walker, was a Sunday school teacher who continued to pour the Word of God into me. She was a beautiful lady, the same age as my mother, and I truly looked up to her. She had a beautiful voice; when she sang, it would shake up the entire church house!

Mr. Walker was the neighborhood mentor. He had a blue truck that he drove through the neighborhood as he mentored and impacted the lives of young boys in our community. Initially, I wasn't very good at sports. However, Mr. Walker placed me on his team and continued to work with me until I became a pretty good player. Our team's name was United Taxi. I often thought Mr. Walker allowed me to be on the team because I was his pastor's kid, however, once he began training us in how to properly throw, catch, and swing a bat, we developed into a really good competitive team. My younger brother, Michael, even started playing with the older boys at the age of 9. He was truly a great player. He later played in the College World Series, became a college All-American, and was invited to try-out for the Houston Astros professional baseball team. I was so proud of him as playing professional baseball had always been a dream of mine.

My elementary years were filled with wonderful childhood memories. My friends and I played football and baseball in the streets and were in the house before the streetlights came on in the evening. We resided in that house on

Wheeler Avenue for the remainder of my childhood.

My father's ministry was expanding as he continued to work a full-time job from 4:30am to 4:30pm daily, Monday through Friday. Because we only had one automobile, I would often ride with my mother to pick him up after work. The picture of a group of tired, weary, mostly African American men covered in sweat and silt is still vividly imprinted in my mind. I watched many of those men walk out of that factory where they had been slaving in 130-degree heat all day just to make a decent living to support their families. Many days, Dad would shower and dress inside the foundry, then visit his parishioners, the sick, and the shut-in. The church continued to grow. Watching my dad's stamina and strength served to give me a work ethic that often seems to be non-stop, even to my own detriment.

After my first year at Avondale Elementary School, I was promoted to the 4th grade. My teacher was Ms. Creasman. I had always been a good student, even though I was not committed to studying. Learning always came easy for me and I was always at the head of, or leader of my class. Desegregation was extremely challenging, as men like Dr. Martin Luther King Jr. and others continued to push for justice and civil rights for all black, poor, and disenfranchised people. However, I was facing my own transitional challenges in the classroom. As a young African American, there were some horrible realities that were right in front of me. I remember two incidents that still bombard my mind.

My sister Gail also attended Avondale and regularly came

home complaining about being bullied by this young white boy. He would pull her hair and call her names. After hearing Gail complain for several days, I decided the next day to ask for permission from my teacher to go to the restroom. My plan was to go by my sister's classroom to see if I could spot any mischief. Low and behold, when I walked by her classroom, there was this boy pulling on her ponytails and calling her the "n-word" just as she had stated. As mentioned previously, I have never liked physical confrontation; however, as a protector of my sister in those very tenuous times, I entered her classroom and began to wail on the head of that kid! The teacher escorted me to the principal's office and of course called my father. I was frightened of my dad's possible response. However, his response was one I will never forget. He said, *"Ternae, I am not advocating violence or fighting, but you did the right thing by protecting your sister."* Those words left a lasting impression in my mind. It made me understand that even though violence is not necessarily right, it is necessary for one to stand and fight for the things you believe in and the rights of those who experience oppression and abuse. The event made a lasting impression on me, and to this day, I still find myself standing up for "the least of these."

This is a lesson that transcends various backgrounds. You never know when you'll be called on for the sake of the fight. The fight could be for better opportunities in the workplace. It could be for acceptance of diversity. It could be for equal pay. It could be for the opportunity to let someone else lead. And there is always a proper way to handle the fight. Sure, you could go in, screaming and demanding what you prefer. But as a leader, as one who will cause others to transform, it's imperative that your example always sets the tone for what's next. Ask yourself what tone you're setting if you always want to fight with your hands and not your intelligence?

The second event that scarred my memory was Ms. Creasman and her dog, Pebbles. I truly believed she loved that dog more than the kids in her own class. Every day after lunch she would set all the students around her feet as she sat in her rocking chair to read us a story. I will always remember this day when she chose a book entitled, "Little Black Sambo." This day as always, she would read a page and then turn the book around and show us the picture on the page. I have no idea why she chose this particular book on that particular day; however, I do know that every time she read a page she would show the picture of a little black boy running through the jungle half naked and every kid sitting at her feet would turn and look at me! I could not quite comprehend the feeling or all the emotions that engulfed me, but I somehow knew something wasn't right. I felt humiliated. I went home that evening and told my dad about Ms. Creasman reading the book with the negative images and how all the kids focused their looks on me. I've never seen my dad so angry. The next day, he went to the school and asked to meet with the principal. After a few choice words, my dad went to the library, removed the book from the shelf, and "Little Black Sambo" never appeared again in the halls or library of Avondale Elementary School.

Here we go again – fighting the right way! My dad could have chosen a physical altercation. After all, he was defending and protecting his seed. However, the leader in him showed up. The advocate in him showed up. Yes, he was the father first; he was also, however, the man who refused to let any ounce of discriminatory innuendos float freely. And if you're ever going to lead a group of people anywhere, you have to be willing to protect them. You have to be willing to, as some would say, "call a spade a spade."

Because of my father's willingness to fight properly, he protected not only me, but other young black boys who would come behind me. He made a bold statement that we were not to be painted improperly and that it would never be allowed as normal. A true leader does that. They identify traces of ill-willed agendas and cut them at the root, dismantling the very power of false persuasiveness before it has the chance to grow.

My 6th grade teacher was Ms. Pennington. I must say, she challenged and pushed me to be the best I could be. She constantly called my mom and dad to let them know that I was not working up to my fullest potential. She truly would get on my nerves. As I look back, while I always made good grades, I also always received an "N" (needs improvement) in conduct. To this day, I still believe I received that grade because any time I felt or saw injustice, I would speak up about it. And while desegregation proved to be a challenge for us students, we also knew that most of our teachers had never encountered teaching black children either. I now thank God for teachers like Ms. Pennington who were willing to push me beyond my comfort zone to use all of my gifts and talents to excel. These experiences truly prepared me for the next transition in my life, Middle School.

Make sure that the push you're giving your team, your associates, today will make them appreciate you more tomorrow. No, they may not always like you. But a leader's job is not to gain popularity; it's to encourage growth.

Chapter 3 Building Blocks

1. Even when dread and despair appear to be around you, try to look at things differently. How can YOU be the catalyst for change? What can YOU bring to the table that causes things to shift for the better?

2. Your words hold weight, yes. But your heart and hands must be trusted as well. Every leader has to ensure that they aren't just "talkers," but "action takers." In taking action, ensure that your intent is always for the greater good and with no hidden agendas.

3. Pay attention to the fights you get invited to. Every battle is not yours to fight, no. However, there are those battles that are depending on you to show up and set the record straight. Protect your character and integrity by choosing to fight well and fight when it's proper. Never out of emotions, but out of necessity for transformation.

4. Respect those who see the greatness in you and will not allow you to get comfortable in mediocrity. When you're challenged to step up and do better, ponder on the reality before promoting an

immature response. Some people will sincerely believe in you and will never let you settle. Honor them and be that for the one coming behind you.

DR. TERNAE JORDAN, SR.

CHAPTER 4

The Middle Passage

Transition always comes with real challenges. Moving from elementary to middle school was like walking into a dark tunnel with no light at the end of it. The world was in turmoil with the war in Vietnam, our country was at war in a place far removed from us, and people of color were wrestling with poverty and injustice here in America. Dr. King, who had been fighting for years for social justice and equity for people of color, was now speaking out on the war in Vietnam. Needless to say, as I entered Hardy Junior High School, which was zoned to include children in our community, little did I know that we were about to enter a tunnel of racism that we had never experienced in our young lives.

Hardy Junior High School was located in East Chattanooga. It was located across the railroad tracks in a community where there were no blacks, and it was also the local home of the Ku Klux Klan. In the fall of 1924, the Chattanooga Board of Commissioners voted its approval for a new junior high school to be built in East Chattanooga, which was known as the 12th Ward. The school was designed to serve two communities; East Chattanooga and Avondale, which were both white because of segregation. The site for the new school was to be named in honor of the mayor of Chattanooga at that time, Richard Hardy. Plans were completed and the building began under the supervision of the then commissioner Frazier and superintendent J.S. Ziegler. The new school was organized in September of 1925. The 9th grade class at that time was sent to Chattanooga High School and the 7th and 8th grade students were divided between Avondale and East Chattanooga elementary schools. The new building was not ready for occupancy that year; however, towards the end of the year, the children from all three schools met in the new gymnasium for a program and to walk through the building. Superintendent Ziegler was present.

In the fall of 1926, the building was completed, occupied, and enrollment was large. The dedication ceremony took place near Thanksgiving in the presence of Mayor Richard Hardy, Commissioner Frazier, Superintendent Ziegler, friends of the school, and the entire student body. Many years later, in 1969, the children from my community prepared to enter this tunnel.

It was obvious that we were not wanted in this new school. As we congregated to walk to school together, we crossed over the railroad tracks and entered a hostile environment where we faced the ugly cruel monster of racism and abuse. We were all frightened as we gathered together going to and from school. Every day, when we crossed the railroad tracks, we came face to face with a gang of white boys led by "Lefty." We called him Lefty because he was a tall, scraggly, red-headed kid, who always met us with a knife held in his left hand. To us, Lefty was our giant Goliath, standing in our way; we were little David in the Bible, simply trying to get an education. Every day, Lefty and his gang were there to torment and chase us all until we reached the other side of the tracks. And when the bell rang to end our school day, a group of us would assemble to walk back toward the railroad tracks, knowing that Lefty and his gang would be waiting for us. We all walked together because we knew that if we walked together and dispersed in many different directions, Lefty and his gang could not attack all of us. As I look back on those times, they were both transitional and traumatizing. To this day, I still have a hard time understanding just how evil and cruel segregation and racism are. It was during that time that my eyes were opened to the fact that people could hate others simply based on their skin color.

Elementary school was a challenge, however crossing this part of the Jordan into middle school was a time that left a lasting impact and scars on my brain that I still struggle with today. As I reflect, the many injustices that I experienced as a child still plague our country and world today. I am overcome with grief and challenged to do everything I can to help people learn to love and live together in peace. My dad always instilled this in me: *"You are no better than anyone else, however, you are as good as anyone else."* His wisdom and guidance always gave me confidence and courage to know who I was in my walk and relationship with God. He taught me to understand that all men, regardless of their skin color or race, are created equal and that we should learn to love one another just as Christ loves us, regardless of who we are or where we come from. My desire has always been to see people loving and living together in unity.

Here is another moment for us to park the car. The quote that my father so graciously and boldly planted in my heart and hearing has been music to my ears in times of doubt. As a leader and as one who is entrusted with a team of any size, it's imperative that we make everyone on our team believe that they can do absolutely anything. In your home, your family should feel encouraged. In the school system, children and educators should feel empowered. In the boardroom, ideas should be birthed that prove ingenuity and creativity. In politics, people should feel seen and heard. No matter who you're leading and where you're leading them to, people are more apt to follow you when they believe that **YOU** believe in them.

As I look back on that middle passage season, I'm grateful to the awesome black teachers, male and female, who helped us maneuver those dark waters and to integrate into this eye-opening world. There were men like Mr. Grady Polk, our school principal, a very proud, stern and strong man; Chief Martin, "the enforcer" who made sure we stayed in line; Mr. Atto Taylor, a very handsome and intelligent young recent college graduate who encouraged, supported and gave us students of color a great sense of pride; Miss Jacqueline Guice, a gym teacher fresh out of Tennessee State University, a historical black college (HBCU); Mr. Malcolm Walker and Mrs. Seay, a beautiful young woman who set a tremendous image for our young black women; Mr. Manns, our band and theater instructor who gave us many opportunities to express ourselves through the Arts. We knew these people were there to be great role models and mentors, and to set good images and great examples as guiding lights for each of us to look up to. They were us, and I'm very grateful to them for pouring their lives into us to prepare us for our next transition into high school.

Seventh grade was an exciting time. It did not take me long to get involved in areas of leadership like student council. I was a natural leader even in those early days. It was not something I sought, but something I seemed to be sucked into. However, sports were another story.

I loved all sports but was only good at one and that was baseball. I can remember going out for football. I was so excited to put on that practice uniform, which by the way was much too big for me. The long pants swallowed me up, the unfitted jersey fell below my wrist, and the big helmet spun around on my small head, making me look like a kid from another planet. However, I also remember running out onto the field with my other classmates looking to become the next Jim Brown, Walter Payton, or Gale Sayers. But, when my coach, Mr. Jay Johnston, who also served as the baseball coach, saw me exit the locker room, he turned around in front of all my friends and classmates and screamed, *"Ternae, what are you doing here? You are not a football player!"* I stood there humiliated, feeling like a weasel that had just had his head decapitated. My spirit was crushed and broken. Needless to say, I was embarrassed. That ended my football career.

Now, that coach may not have understood the importance

of our words; but that day, his words crushed the possibility of success for me in another sport. As a leader, have you ever killed someone's abilities with your words? Let this be a powerful example of how and why we must be careful with what we release through our words. You never know just how long the impact will last. Even if someone may not be the greatest at a particular thing, focus on their strengths and find a way to communicate other possibilities for them. Using shame and embarrassment tactics never go over well. Don't be that type of leader – in or out of the home.

Basketball was another story. We had some of the best basketball players in the city of Chattanooga attend Hardy. Guys like Anthony McAfee, Edward Earl Stewart, Jeffery and Michael Poole, and who could forget Anthony "Woosie" Roberts – who received a scholarship to Oral Roberts University. He became the second leading scorer in the nation and was later drafted by the Denver Nuggets in the first round. He then went on to become the Rookie of the Year. He was undoubtedly one of the best basketball players to ever come out of Chattanooga. However, baseball was truly my sport.

I'm very proud to say that, as a 9th grader, I became "Mr. Baseball" for Hardy Junior High School. That was my male, masculine moment in middle school. To be honored and walk away with that trophy presented by baseball coach Jay Johnson, the same coach Johnson who rejected and humiliated me earlier in my football days, was validating. It felt so good to redeem myself and to come out on top, when others did not believe in me. It's a powerful irony how the very ones who doubt your ability will have to see you persevere and reward you for not giving up.

As I shared earlier, I was always a good student who usually ended up on the honor roll. However, in middle school, my interest began to shift from my studies to girls. They became my fascination. I believe it was because I grew up next door to the five Tolliver girls in my early years. It always seemed easier for me to connect to the female species. In fact, all of my life, most of my friends were female, whether at home, church, or school.

One of the most defining moments of middle school was when it was announced that we would have a talent show. Again, be reminded that I always loved to sing. There were many performers that I admired during those days; groups like The Temptations, Dells, Stylistics, Chi-lites, Temprees, Manhattans, Spinners, Smokey Robinson & the Miracles, as well as single artists like Stevie Wonder and many others. My secret dream was to be a part of one of those groups. I loved the way they would work a crowd and the response the crowd would give back to them. It was phenomenal! I did have the opportunity to become part of the Memphis Tempress while I was in college, but I was afraid of what my parents would think, after I had already completed three years of college. But my favorite group at the time was actually The Jackson 5, who burst on the scene in 1964. They were five brothers out of Gary, Indiana with a "bubblegum" soul flavor. Man, they had "swag" and were managed by their very domineering and demanding father, Joe Jackson. These young men were very talented and had a younger brother named Michael who was the real star, making all the girls swoon. So why not, if you wanted to impress the girls, imitate Michael Jackson?

I chose to be part of the talent show as Michael Jackson and to sing his hit, "Who's Loving You?" The song had taken the charts by storm, and everyone was mesmerized by this young man's talent, so I decided that if I was going to be in the show I had to be the epitome of who Michael was. I remember that night like it was yesterday. There was so much excitement in the place. The house was packed, standing room only. When my name was called, I walked out onto that stage and blew the roof off the place. The audience went wild! After that night, all of the young ladies wanted to be my friend. I became one of the big men on campus. That talent show was so well received that another junior high invited us to perform our Tiger talent show at their school. The name of the school was Alton Park Middle.

Alton Park Middle School was one of our greatest crosstown rivals. I was excited and felt like a movie star. Sitting in the audience the day I performed was a beautiful young lady who was a friend of a girl who attended my dad's church. Her name was Angela Faye Smith. Angela lived next door to Sandra Reid. Her father was a deacon at our church. When Sandra heard we were going to perform at Alton Park, she told Angela to be on the lookout for her Pastor's son, who was none other than - you guessed it, me - Ternae Tsargaris Jordan. She told her I would sing "Who's Loving You," by the Jackson 5. I need to stick a pin at this moment because Angela Faye Smith will later become a very significant part of my life forever.

It's amazing how you can simply be at the right place, at the right time, and connect with someone who will partner with your destiny. This is another powerful leadership nugget, which proves how proximity can lead to progression and prosperity. Remember, prosperity is about more than finances; having prosperous relationships is a major element in one's success and longevity.

Chapter 4 Building Blocks

1. Don't ever forget that you belong in the room of success just as much as the next person. A real leader honors the shine of others and refuses to compete.

2. Your belief in someone else can help them learn to believe in themselves. Leaders are constantly letting their teams know that they see and appreciate what they bring to the table. Never let them feel like they are insignificant.

3. Proximity can lead to progressions and prosperity. Don't be afraid to shift locations. It can be the difference between your success today and your exponential increase tomorrow.

4. Don't let your words or your attitude be the dream killer for someone else. Even when you don't like what you see, be careful how you identify it. One wrong look or move can cause someone to give up.

DR. TERNAE JORDAN, SR.

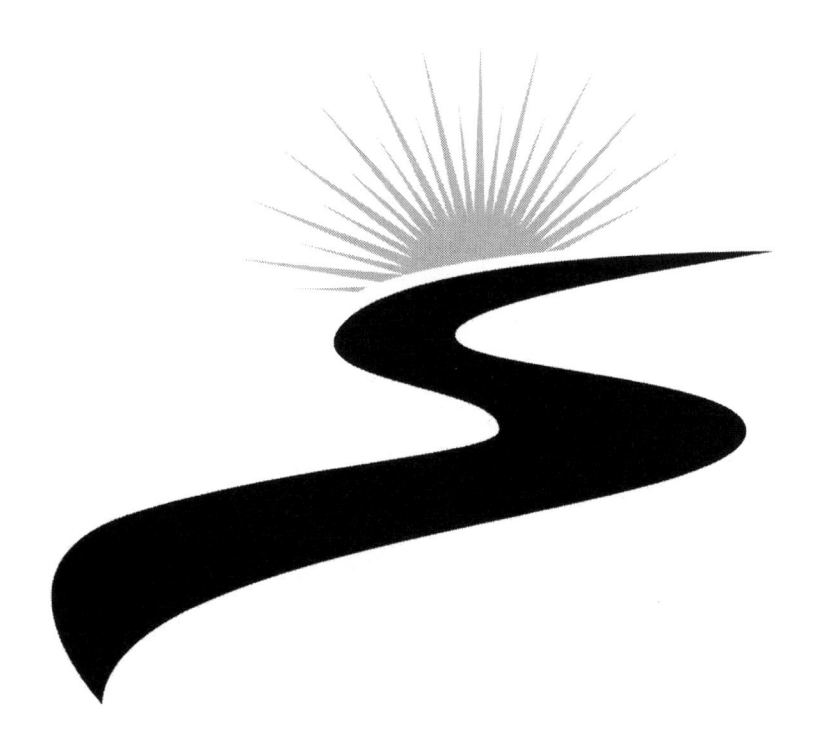

CHAPTER 5

The Next Passage

In May of 1970, I graduated from Hardy Junior High School. I was finally ready for the big time and the next major transition in my life: High School. It was a time of major turbulence in schools across the country. The winds of desegregation were blowing high. The school I was zoned to attend was Brainerd High School, however there had been major riots there during 1969 and the early parts of the 70's. I shared with you previously that I had always tried to avoid confrontation and violence at all costs, so I had no desire to attend Brainerd. I decided to enroll in Chattanooga High School which was known as City High. It was located on the other side of town.

Desegregation seemed to have gone much smoother at Chattanooga High. Perhaps, it was because its location was in an integrated neighborhood where black and white kids had grown up together. To attend this school, I had to get up at 5am every morning to catch the bus at 6am, go to downtown Chattanooga, then transfer to another bus headed to North Chattanooga, which was located across the Tennessee River. North Chattanooga was an interesting close-knit community where many years later I would pastor my first church.

My 10th grade year was relatively smooth. I made many friends, including some whom I would later pastor. Nothing too impactful happened during that first year. However, as the conversation about desegregation continued to grab the headlines and the political debate continued to escalate, my 11th grade year was far different. I was forced by the Chattanooga public school system to enroll in Brainerd High School. In September of 1970, I walked into the halls of Brainerd with a conflicted heart and mind. I had no idea the impact attending this school, with its traumatic history, would have on my future. I was nervous, bewildered, and afraid. I knew this transition, this next river that I would cross, would be the one that would lead me into my life defining moments. I had successfully transitioned the river of elementary school and had successfully crossed the river of middle school, even with the storms I faced in those places. However, I knew that whatever happened in the next two years would either make or break me, as I moved from my preparation years into adulthood. They would determine my future. With much anxiety, I launched into a new space. Little did I know that what would transpire the next two days would propel me into the future that God had already prepared for me from birth. Brainerd High School, with all of its challenges, proved to be one of the best things that ever happened to me. My favorite Bible verse Romans 8:28 (KJV) says, *"And we know that all things work together for good to them that love God, to them who are the called according to his purpose."*

Now, you know we have to talk about this. As leaders, how many times have we complained about being relocated? Reassigned? Relaunched in another area? The truth is that we do NOT enjoy change. Comfortability is preferred more than inevitability; however, those inevitable changes can often be the greatest shift for our success and maturity. When you're being groomed to lead, you have to be willing to go where you don't want to go sometimes. It's in those locations that you find what you needed all along.

I have journeyed through the past years, and I am now crossing Jordan again. God used me spiritually. I spoke and sang for church youth groups, despite being determined not to be a minister or preacher. I truly loved God and believed I could serve him by singing, praying, and speaking, but I made up my mind I would never accept the call that I knew he had placed on my life. Growing up in a pastor's home I knew the expectations, spotlight, and scrutiny, along with rejection and pain of everyone else's opinions for a man of God. Imperfect people expect you not to make mistakes or fall short. I desired to escape that place and that position. As a child, it was embarrassing for me to be among children who were doing the things that young people did, yet I never engaged in or had a desire to participate. Ironically, my peers seemed to respect and admire this young man that never went to parties, never smoked cigarettes or marijuana that was running freely in the early 70's. What was it about me that set me apart, yet connected me to those that I was around? I now know it was a mantle that I did not desire to wear, yet by the grace of God I wore it with class, confidence, and humility. It was in this place that I would meet an elderly woman from Alabama who would impact and change my life forever. Most times, we don't want to accept or embrace what's on us. But when you are called to lead, called to transform, you can't fight it.

On the first day of class at Brainerd High, I picked up my schedule. My schedule included a class called "D.E." I truly got excited. What 16 year old young man did not want to be in a Driver Education class? Every young person wanted their driver's license. Lucky me! I was in a class that would do just that. However, when I walked into the class there stood this short, 5'4" elderly white woman named Fleta Hull. It did not take me long to figure out that D.E. was not driver's education. Instead, it was a class called "Distributive Education," which taught leadership and career development to young people. The goal was to prepare them for leadership in the work world. Public speaking happened to be one of the core class components. Speaking before crowds had never been a problem for me. I grew up speaking two and three times a Sunday for youth groups in different churches across our city. While I was comfortable with this class, I now find it ironic that it was a necessary component in my becoming the man and leader I am today.

The first assignment given on that first day of class was to prepare a speech. Most people know that speaking in public is usually the number one fear for many. That night, I began to think about what I would speak about before I dropped the class the next day. The concerns I had at that time were about the Civil Rights Movement and desegregation. Dr. Martin Luther King, Jr. had been assassinated two years earlier in 1968 while standing on the balcony of the Lorraine Motel in Memphis, Tennessee. In 1963, before he died, he delivered the speech, "I Have a Dream" on the steps of the Lincoln Memorial in Washington DC. He reminded me of my father whom I greatly admired. So, what better speech to deliver than the one that was a great concern of these two giants. That evening, I stayed up late preparing a speech that would be a staple for my future and a catapulting force moving forward.

The next morning as I entered the classroom, I found out that every kid in the class had decided to drop the class. I had decided to do the same. But, when it was my time to speak, I stood behind the podium, lifted my shoulders, stuck out my chest, and spoke clearly and distinctly about something I truly believed all my life: that all men are created equal and therefore we should love one another and learn to live together in unity. When I finished, I sat down. To my amazement, the mesmerized class gave me a standing ovation! I was embarrassed and could not wait for the bell to ring to get out of there. When it did ring, I sprinted toward the door, but Ms. Hull cornered me. This woman reminded me of an old southern woman who conjured up negative emotions like that of my 4th grade teacher, Miss Creasman, who had scarred and traumatized my life. However, to my surprise, Mrs. Hull walked up to me, placed her hand on my shoulders, and simply said,

"Ternae, you have a gift for speaking." Those words coming from this southern white woman on the second day of class at Brainerd High impacted and encouraged me, thus setting me on a course that would become an awesome ride as I headed toward the completion of my high school career. Her acknowledgement of my gift helped to shape and mold me. It takes a real leader to identify someone's gift. She could have made me feel worthless. She could have brushed off what had just occurred. She could have responded in a plethora of other ways. However, the leader in her recognized the leader in me; therefore, she used that moment to affirm me. That was a very powerful display of respect, compassion, and belief. That speech about loving people in spite of what was going on in our world, set me on a path in which I wholeheartedly and sincerely believed. Despite the racism in our country and the war raging in our world, God somehow allowed this woman to light a fire in me. The subject of racism and loving people, despite who they were, became my passion. I found out that my voice had power, my words could make a difference, and my gift could help empower people to change the world for the better. Those words of encouragement changed my world forever and assured me my gift could make room for me.

My junior year exploded. God was truly using me in my church and educational life, even against my own will. I was in a strange place. Ministry was not my desire. I loved people and always wanted to help them but did not want to preach. It was a crazy dilemma, a spiritual and emotional tug of war was going on in my head, yet there was one thing I knew I could not escape. I knew, like Joseph in the Bible, that the Lord was with me. If He created me and purposed me to carry His word, I was destined to do just that. I had no choice if I truly wanted to live a peaceful, purposeful, and successful life. I dove deeper into the Distributive Education world Ms. Hull exposed me to and she promoted me anyway she could as one of her most prized possessions. My world was about to explode.

Distributive Education had a club called "DECA," which stands for the Distributive Education Club of America. Different schools would compete with other clubs throughout the city and state. Through my involvement with DECA I was introduced to an awesome man who would become a mentor, friend and colleague, Mr. Samuel Trammell. He was the director of Distributive Education for the Chattanooga school system. He and Ms. Hull saw golden nuggets and diamonds in me. They pushed and propelled me into being one of the best high school public speakers in our city. I competed and won 1st place District, City, State, and even National awards in the field of public speaking. I was also selected to be a delegate to the national convention two years in a row in Chicago and Atlantic City. I was also selected as the DECA state parliamentarian for the State of Tennessee and traveled throughout the state during the school year, training and encouraging other young leaders to take advantage of this awesome program that meant so much to me. This club truly changed my life and gave me leadership skills that I would use for the rest of my life.

Another component of the Distributive Education program was called "Co-op." It allowed students the opportunity to take core classes in the morning and work as an apprentice on various jobs in the afternoon. Being one of the leading students in our class, I was blessed to be placed as a student salesman in one of the leading department stores in our city. In the mid-60s, blacks were only allowed to do minor jobs in downtown stores and were not allowed to eat at lunch counters. There were student sit-ins happening across the south. Even in our city, students from our all-black school, Howard High, were staging walkouts and sit-in protests.

It was rare for a young 16 year old black kid to be placed on the sales floor of a leading department store to engage and interact with customers. This was so exciting to me. Someone believed in me enough to allow me to take a premier sales position, get a grade, get paid, and learn leadership skills all at once. Man was I blessed! Of course, Ms. Hull, my job coordinator, had forged a great relationship with employers all over the city of Chattanooga. She highly recommended me and followed my progress. Her faith in me helped build my self-esteem and in turn, my confidence soared through the roof. I was living a high school junior's dream. Working a full-time job, making good grades, dating one of the prettiest young ladies in school, being a leader in my high school, and later becoming the first African American senior class president. What more could one ask for? It all seemed like a storybook journey to me.

In crossing rivers on the journey of life, one must also cross many ditches, mistakes, and bad choices. It did not take me very long to realize that even when you are soaring high, temptation is always present to bring you down. My parents taught me at an early age that it takes a lifetime to build a good name and only a second to destroy it. My understanding of this was forged on the sales floor of Loveman's Department Store. As a junior, I was doing great in school and at my job. However, while working there, I encountered an older African American woman who happened to be a full-time employee. She latched on to me. One day, during the Christmas holiday rush, she approached me and said, *"Ternae, I want to show you how to make some good extra money."* She began to tell me about a scheme that she used. Whenever she made a sale during the holiday rush, if someone had the exact cash and tax due, she would simply take their money, which she assured the customer she would deposit in the cash register, then place their items in a bag. But, once the customer left, she would then put the cash in her pocket. Of course, this was something that I would never consider. This was totally against my character, reputation, and upbringing. This is where I learned that the enemy, when he cannot get you to succumb the first time, will never give up. He constantly continues to attack you. I always heard that the devil comes to kill, to steal, and to destroy; however, being a person of faith, it is easy to believe that temptation and the enemy cannot get next to you. After rejecting her offer day after day, she continued to pursue and share with me how much money she was making. We have to be careful that we don't let anyone take away our good character and ability to make the right decision. In the blink of an eye, things can plummet if you're not aware and confident in the foundation of truth.

One day, when we were extremely busy on the sales floor, a woman came in to buy cufflinks as a Christmas gift. As always, I was friendly and cheerful with her as she purchased the gift and handed me the exact change. I thanked her, as I did with each customer. After she left, I headed toward the cash register to deposit the money. There was a line of sales people standing in line ringing up their customer purchases. As I continued to stand in line, I heard this voice in my head say: *"Pocket the money; no one is looking."* In my spirit and in my head I kept telling myself, *"NO!"* I knew that true character is what one is when no one is watching. However, at the same time, I was hearing in my head how much money the older saleswoman was making. I'm embarrassed to say that after I looked around to see if anyone was looking, I put the money in my pocket and went back to the sales floor to make more sales. I was nervous and very uncomfortable and somehow knew I was making a decision that could have an impact on my reputation and my future.

Two hours later I looked up and saw a man coming down the escalator towards me. As he approached me, he said, *"Ternae, I am the store detective. Would you follow me upstairs to the office, please?"* I was devastated on my march toward that office. All I could think of was what would Ms. Hull think? What will I tell my friends? What are my mother and father going to say? This had to be the worst predicament and feeling I've ever felt in my life. On the march toward what seemed like my demise, the detective led me into a small interrogation room and closed the door. He pulled up a chair and leaned towards me. My heart was pumping so hard I thought it would jump out of my chest. My hands were shaking, and my knees were about to buckle under me. I saw visions of me being arrested, handcuffed, led through the store to the backseat of a police cruiser, and then carted off to prison for some ungodly prison sentence. I could hear my father's voice ringing in my ear, *"Ternae, it takes a lifetime to build up a name and one second to destroy it."* Lord, what had I done?

I could see my whole future passing before my eyes, but what actually happened next became another *Kairos* (God) moment and a turning point in my life. The detective looked at me and said, *"We have been losing sales and money has been disappearing lately. Today, we caught you on camera stealing."* What? This was the first time I ever performed this act and now I'm being charged with all the losses that the store has been incurring. It was at that moment that I realized I had taken the bait. The friend, or should I say so-called friend that had been encouraging me to perform this outrageous act had set me up to take the fall for all that she had been doing. Now I'm devastated. I failed myself, my teacher, my school, and my parents by listening to the wrong voice in my head. I thought it was over! But what happened next got my attention. The detective leaned in, looked me straight in the eye and uttered these words: *"Ternae, there are two kinds of people in the world; one who makes a mistake and continues down that path, and one that makes a decision, then turns around and heads in the other direction."* And as he continued to gaze into my eyes he asked the second question: *"What kind of person are you?"* This had to be the most challenging question I had ever been asked. It was at that moment that I came to grips with my inner soul Ternae. What kind of person are you "really?" I was embarrassed. I had failed. I was wounded, traumatized, and hurt, but more than anything I was devastated to have a (white) man look me in the eye and question my character and integrity. At that moment, I made up my mind that never again would another human being be able to look me in the eye and question who I am. Yes, I was guilty, but I knew I would never do anything like that ever again. I really learned two lessons that day. I now had evidence of the statement my dad had always shared about my name and reputation. However, I also learned that there are people who are around you who will do anything they can to destroy your name in order to make themselves look better. God, I thank you so much for this lesson on my journey crossing the river of knowledge, wisdom, and the truth of Your Word. The word says trust no man; only love and honor them. I learned this lesson the hard way that day.

Leaders, during any part of their growth journey, will always have their integrity tested. Sometimes, it's with an evil agenda behind it. Other times, it's to show you what's really inside of you. And from the story I just shared, integrity also is rooted in whether or not you'll be willing to play the blame game. You see, I had the opportunity to tell what my co-worker had been doing. But the fact of the matter is that I, too, was guilty – even if it was one time. Therefore, I had to take responsibility for my own actions and be grateful that the scenario didn't go another way. To be honest, it should have. In life and in leadership, accountability is necessary.

Growing up was challenging and not all things were good. However, looking back on my teenage years, despite the racism we faced and an occasional youthful wrong decision, I believe the halls of Brainerd High were some of the best years of my life. It was there I finally connected with the young lady of my dreams, fell in love, and began one of the most beautiful love stories that I have ever experienced.

Brainerd High School was where Angela Smith, the young lady that I had been trying to impress for so long, and I connected. The year I arrived she was a sophomore. Once we connected, we were together all the time. We never ate lunch in the lunchroom. We would always get an ice cream sandwich and head to the school patio to spend our time together. Who needs food? We were two crazy kids who were finding love for the first time. When I met Angela, I knew she was something special. Her mother and father, Lillian and Sidney Smith, were great people. Her father served as a deacon at the Westside Baptist Church in Chattanooga, where I would speak and sing from time to time. Her parents were very strict and would not allow us to connect early on. Angela's family also consisted of two brothers; Sidney Jr. and Timothy Douglas, along with three sisters; Mary Ann, Denise, and Susan. When I first started coming around, Denise was already away at the University of Michigan and Susan was at Howard University in Washington D.C. Mary Ann was married and already raising her own family.

After meeting Angela's parents, they were convinced that this guy, Ternae, was different and that maybe he would not be such a bad influence on their daughter. They eventually welcomed me into their lives and their home. It's amazing that when God is with you in every facet, season, and level of growth in your life, He walks with you and gives you favor. Angela was a God-fearing young lady. She was beautiful, sweet, and liked by everyone. I had many friends, mostly girls, but I knew the first time I laid eyes on her that she had this special character that led me to believe she would be my soulmate. I adored her even then and could see us connecting for life and having a wonderful family.

We dated all through high school. She would often go with me when I gave speeches at local events and church services. Angela became my "ride or die" friend. She was an encouragement and supported me in everything I did. Every day we would sit, laugh, play, and even have special, secret conversations about marriage. We were just two crazy teenagers growing up trying to find our way, but knowing that in order to have a successful, fulfilling life, we both believed we had to have God in our life.

Those high school years moved by fast. Between work, my love life, speaking engagements, school, and family, I stayed pretty active and busy. I became a pretty popular guy on campus in spite of my casual presence in my senior year of 1972-1973. I was voted as the first African American senior class president that Brainerd High School ever had. That was pretty cool. I would say considering the era and time of racial strife we were in, knowing that I was respected enough by both black and white students to lead their class was an honor. Never take it lightly when people can look beyond cultural barriers and respect the gift that is in you. People don't have to like or support you; when they do, gratitude should always follow, and humility should always lead you.

As the year drew to a close, seniors were considering what college they would attend. I had never given much thought to what I would do after graduation. Again, I felt like I had no choice because it was clear, from the strong tug I felt, that if God had predestined my life for ministry then I had no other option. One day, Ms. Hull asked me, *"Ternae, what do you plan to do after high school?"* I asked myself, *"What high school student knows what they want to do or become?"* I had no plans, so I answered, *"I want to do for others what you have done for me. I want to teach and train young people and become a Distributive Education teacher."* She stared back at me and asked me, *"Do you really?"* And because I had no other answer, I simply said, *"Yes ma'am."* She replied, *"Ternae I am getting close to retirement. If you think you want to become a Distributive Education teacher, I will hold on until you graduate, and I will give you my job."* In my mind I was thinking, but said out loud, *"Sure, Ms. Hull. You will wait four years for me to graduate so you can give me your job."* She responded, *"I will."*

In September 1973, I headed off to the University of Tennessee in Knoxville to major in Marketing and Distributive Education. Like every other high school graduate heading into their first year of college, I was both excited and nervous. First of all, I had never lived away from my parents and the excitement of living on my own and not having anyone tell me what I could and couldn't do sounded exciting. However, because I had been such a church boy all my life, I was concerned how I would react to being on my own, attending parties (which I had never done), and how I would manage school work since I had always been a good student, but had never totally applied myself in academics. High school was a breeze, but now I would have to manage my own time and life. The test of a true leader comes when they are left to their own devices, but still choose to do what honors their destiny.

I will always remember the day my mom and dad dropped me off at the University of Tennessee. As we unloaded the car and took my few belongings up to my dorm room, I could see that my dad was so proud, yet I could also see the tears and the concern in my mom's eyes, knowing that she was dropping off her first born who was quickly becoming a man. As they were about to pull out, there was a lump that began to form in my throat. Mom hugged me and headed to the car so that she would not break down crying. I remember dad turning around and saying, *"Ternae, we have tried to raise you in the right way. You are a man now and your own decisions will determine your future, so please make the right choices."* As they got into the automobile and pulled off, I finally realized that I was now a man, on my own, and I needed to make the best of it. My future would literally depend on it.

College was exciting. I remember the great Saturday afternoon football games. I fell in love with the Tennessee Vols and never missed a game. Condridge Holloway, the first African American quarterback in the Southeast Conference, entered school the same year I did. He was truly a great football player out of Huntsville, Alabama, where all of my relatives lived. I also came in with the great Ernie Grunfeld, an awesome basketball player out of New York, who would later team up with Bernard King to make our basketball team one of the best in the country. I've loved these two sports my entire life. And it wasn't until I entered the University of Tennessee that I experienced my first college games.

I received a Work Study Pell Grant job to help pay for my schooling. My job was working with the world famous Pride of the Southland Band. Each week, we would change out the musical scores and the pre and half time shows for the band's performances. This gave me a good inside look at the tremendous amount of work that was put into having an excellent show. The band director, Dr. Julian, was a stern and difficult person to work with; however, his drive for perfection to be the best truly rubbed off on me, showing me what excellence looks like, and that we should always perform to our best ability. Again, another leadership nugget. Regardless of how difficult you think someone might be, be willing to gain what you can. Another southern saying that can help you understand this is *"chew the meat and spit out the bones."* Some people who are trusted to lead have a different way of doing it; however, if you look closely, you'll see that their way isn't bad at all. Misunderstood, possibly. But it always gets the necessary messages across.

Initially, I had quite a few business and marketing classes. As I was filling out my schedule for my sophomore year, I noticed a Black Religious Studies class in the catalog. I knew that this could be an easy "A" for me. After all, I grew up in the Black Church and was an avid Bible scholar, so this could possibly be an easy elective for me. The day that I walked into this class, I was blown away. In front of the class was our instructor, Dr. Riggins Earl. This young professor had a long beard, a tam on his head, a very deep booming voice, and smoked a pipe. In the 70's, there were a lot of hippies and beatniks. This young man fit the image of everything that I had seen on TV, except he was black. I thought he and I would get all the white students educated about the black race together. I thought we could truly make a difference.

As I look back, I realize that encountering this professor became an anchor in the transformation of how I would come to view the world. Dr Earl enlightened and opened up my mind, allowing me to see how religion played a part in the history of the black race, not just in America, but also from the foundation of the world, biblical history even before we left the continent of Africa. He taught me that the white man did not bring us salvation nor religion; we have always been a spiritual and religious people. He taught us how the white race misused religion to support their unsubstantiated claim that the white race is superior. He also taught us that the Garden of Eden was located on the continent of Africa. The word "human being" (that God created), means "man of color." After my encounter with this genius, my life would never be the same.

"Riggins" and I became good friends, but not without much struggle. To this day, he remains a mentor and a friend. I recognized him to be one of the most intelligent, intellectual Black men I had ever encountered. He saw me as a young black man who refused to accept the status quo. He admired me as a student who was thoughtful and energetic enough to research things for himself. Riggins would challenge me before the class and laugh at me in class, which only angered me that much more. My inquisitiveness and his responses led to much anger but built in me the drive to not accept the status quo. One day I told him that the stuff he was teaching us was not the truth. Because of my love, admiration, and the ingenuity of my own father, I challenged Riggins to allow my dad to come to our class. He gladly accepted and scheduled a day for my father to teach. I could not wait for Dad to get there. I wanted to show Riggins and the class that some of the concepts that he was sharing were against everything that I had ever been taught and I knew my dad would be able to substantiate my stance. However, from the moment Riggins and dad met, they hit it off which immediately served to piss me off. Even more, I just knew my dad would correct the misconceptions Riggins was teaching. However, I learned that day that history and black history are different things being taught.

Sometimes, it takes another leader to come in and show us how to understand a point over proving a point. As badly as I wanted my father to prove that I was right, that was not his concern. His only position was to hear and heed to the truth, while knowing how to separate which truths belonged to which issues. That's an amazing leadership trait to carry. If you want to prove anything, stop focusing on proving it. That will make you more of an asset to history.

The word "history" means "his- story." That day, I learned that he who writes the book tells "his-story" and that true American and world history has been distorted to make the writer the hero, consequently alienating others and distorting other races' history. There has been an organized strategy to alienate other races of people and systematically paint them as inferior, primitive, and ignorant people, while highlighting their own stories of history and religion of the white race to substantiate their own claims of white supremacy. This awareness became another stone of remembrance that I was able to pick out of the river, as I continued my journey across the Jordan. It helped me better understand who I am and the role that God created for me to empower, encourage, and educate all God's people to recognize that he is the lover and sustainer of us all.

I thank God for placing Riggins Earl and Melvin Jordan in my life. They are truly my heroes and patriots that God used to open my eyes to a whole new perspective of the gospel message and His plans for all of His people.

Any great leader is willing to learn from others in an effort to respect others. While you may not always agree, strive to understand, and let your differences be a compass for your destiny.

Chapter 5 Building Blocks

1. While we desire to be comfortable, growth does not occur there. Oftentimes, we will have to do what we don't "feel" like doing and go where we don't "feel" like going so that we can accomplish what we need to accomplish. Don't fight the inevitability of maturity in leadership.

2. A leader really can't ignore what's in them and what's on them. You will either release it properly or battle with it until it's free. The best thing to do is "it" – whatever your "it" might consist of.

3. The saying that your "word is your bond" is vital.

Never let anyone or anything cause your words (or actions) to be made out as evil or malicious. Be sure that you are careful about how you represent yourself – even when you don't think anyone is watching.

4. You can prove a point all day, but it takes a mature leader to make sure the point is understood and even received. Don't be so stuck on being right that you're alone in your *rightness*.

5. There is something we can learn from everyone. No matter how ill and difficult you may feel someone is, chew the meat and spit out the bones. In other words, get what you can and discard what doesn't apply.

DR. TERNAE JORDAN, SR.

CHAPTER 6

The Return to Egypt

In the spring of 1977, six months short of my graduation, I returned to Chattanooga to visit my family. While in town, I decided to visit my old alma mater, Brainerd High School, to check in on Ms. Hull. When I walked through the door of her classroom that day, she embraced me with a warm hug of admiration and emotion. This woman, who had invested so much in me, and who had given me so much strength and encouragement to endure, was now embracing me with the love and embrace that only a mother could give.

After welcoming me, she inquired, *"How much longer do you have before you graduate?"* At the time, I was six credit hours short of finishing my college degree. When I told her, she immediately replied, *"Ternae, I'm tired and I'm ready to retire now. I've been waiting all these years for you to finish; however, I can no longer go on. If you promise me that you will return to school this next semester and finish your degree, I will speak with the superintendent and my division head to see if I can get you approved to start teaching now."* What! I could not believe my ears. This woman who believed in me and had been such a blessing of encouragement in my life was now willing to step up and speak up, in order for me to fulfill a promise made years before. She gave me my start in the work world and now she was willing to put her name on the line to give me the start to my career in the area of education.

A vital part of leading is preparing the next generation of leaders coming up behind you. Not only did this teacher impart wisdom and opportunity into me, but she also identified a readiness within me that I had no idea was present. Had she not taken the step to put me in position, I probably would have waited to take her spot. I would have never, in a million years, considered myself ready. But a real leader will not let you delay when destiny is knocking. Take a moment and consider who you may need to go back to and thank. Who poured into you during a time when there was an unknown drought?

She taught me how to appreciate those who believe; not just in you, but in the possibility of you. We often focus on our own aspirations and achievements. We set goals, work to attain them, and strive to prove ourselves to the world. While self-motivation is essential, it is equally crucial to recognize and appreciate the individuals who believe in us along the way and cause us to shift at a moment's notice. These individuals provide unwavering support, acting as pillars of strength during times of transition. And one of the greatest lessons they teach is the potency of belief.

Belief can propel us forward, even in the face of the unknown. When someone believes in your potential, they are investing in your success. Understand that their belief stems from a genuine understanding of your capabilities and an unwavering faith in your ability to achieve greatness. Just as others have believed in you, it is essential to pay it forward and believe in others. Cultivate a culture of support and empowerment within your circles. Take the time to recognize the potential in your colleagues and subordinates, providing them with the guidance and encouragement they need to thrive.

As I look back over my life, it is apparent that God has always placed certain people in my life at certain stages to help propel me into my next season. I have learned not to take those moments and those people for granted. As I've traveled life's journey, I've always felt that I had the anointing of Joseph in my life. No matter what season I am in, whether it's a season of dryness, pruning or fruitfulness, the favor of God has always been there supporting me. I'm coming to realize that like Joseph in every situation the Bible records, *"But God was with Joseph."* I thank you, God, for always being with Ternae.

Chapter 6 Building Blocks

1. Make sure that your delay is not laced in doubt. Oftentimes, your destiny is waiting on you to merely show up, but your excuses will keep you in the bondage of time. Don't allow that to be so!

2. As you lead others, let them know that you believe in them. Whether or not they believe in themselves (at that moment) is irrelevant. Sometimes, your belief has to be borrowed until theirs is strong and sharp enough. Pour your belief onto them and into them. It'll come back to you.

3. Pay attention to those around you. Don't have your head so far in your own world that you ignore the power of those around you.

CROSSING JORDAN

DR. TERNAE JORDAN, SR.

CHAPTER 7

The Love of My Life

I started my teaching career in the Chattanooga public school system at 21 years old. I was only three and a half years removed from my high school graduation. Now, I'm returning to teach at the same school where I received my academic education. Coming back to my own community and the same high school created many challenges that I was ready to face. Many of my first students were young people that I had known all my life. I grew up with them in the community and church. They were accustomed to calling me by my first name, "Ternae." While I was very comfortable with my students calling me by my first name, my principal, Mr. Whittaker, was not and insisted that they call me "Mr. Jordan." Needless to say, this became a challenge for many of them, namely my brother and cousin.

At this time, I was once again living in my parents' house along with my siblings. My brother and I would wake up each morning, get dressed in the same bathroom, and then ride to the same school together. Michael and my cousin, Curtis Jordan, were in my first class. They both were determined not to call me "Mr. Jordan." After all, they had known me all their lives; I was only 21 years old while most of my students were 18 years old. I truly understood their dilemma; however, Mr. Whittaker insisted that all students address the staff as Mr., Ms., or Mrs. as a sign of respect. My brother Michael and cousin Curtis continued to refuse to call me Mr. Jordan. However, I had to invoke my "enforcer" dad, Melvin Jordan, to intervene in order to keep me out of trouble with my superiors. I will never forget having to address this matter with my father and the disdain that I received from Michael and Curtis. After all, I was only Ternae.

This is another major issue in leadership when people cannot respect who you are because they're used to you being who you were. Yes, my brother and cousin had the right to feel how they felt. And maybe you've encountered people on your job or in your family with this same issue. However, you have to be okay - as a leader - with embracing the distinction of you. In some arenas, I may just be Ternae. In other arenas, while I'm aware that *Ternae* is my first name, that is not an acceptable way to address me. Think of any of our presidents; regardless of how you feel about them, they are addressed as Mr. President. I'm certain that no one was walking up to President George Washington, especially in a public political place, and referring to him by first name. And while many had an issue with President Barack Obama, he was still Mr. President. The judge in any courtroom will not be greeted by their first name. In fact, doing so could come with costly reprimands.

The point is that you must first embrace the office you're operating in. And when others want to minimize it, you can explain why that's not acceptable, but you must never accept disrespect that comes after an explanation has been given.

Moving along, the major reason I hurried through college was simple: I was in love with the beautiful young lady that I planned to make my wife.

Angela and I had been dating through high school and college. My plan was to finish school as soon as possible and get a job so that I could make her my wife. She was beautiful, eloquent, and classy. She had a radiating spirit of love and was beautiful inside and out. She was raised in a wonderful home with a loving mother and father. Not only was she beautiful; I knew she truly loved me. During our time dating throughout high school and college, she was loving and supportive. I loved the way she walked. I loved the way she talked. During college I wrote her a letter every day and she reciprocated with a letter to me. I had other friends, but Angela was my heartbeat. I knew from the moment I met her that she was meant to be my wife. Many people don't believe in love at first sight, but I must be honest; it was that way for me. We talked about marriage often; however, her mother would not allow her to attend the same college that I attended. She started out at Tuskegee Institute, an Historical Black College in Tuskegee, Alabama, known for its world famous Tuskegee Airmen and the great Booker T. Washington Carver. He was a Black man born into slavery yet went on to become one of the most influential voices for people of color during the 19th century.

Angela spent her freshman year in Alabama and then transferred to Morris Brown College, another Historical Black College located in Atlanta, Georgia. She was now closer to home.

We became engaged and started planning for our upcoming wedding in June of 1977. I had always dreamed that when I got married, I would ask my wife's father for her hand in marriage. After purchasing an engagement ring, I decided to make an appointment with Mr. Smith. I will always remember his response the day I asked him for Angela's hand in marriage, *"Ternae, why do you want to marry my daughter?"* My reply was, *"Because I love her."* The response he gave in return also still rings in my ear (and I have shared this with every married couple I have counseled since). He said, *"Ternae, I think you are a nice young man and if you and Angela want to get married, you have my blessings. But you don't love her."* The response blew my mind, but his next words I have found to be true: *"You don't love someone until you live with them."* I had no idea what he meant. I knew he did not agree with people living together before marriage. But now, I know what he meant. You don't truly love someone until you've been with them at their best and seen them at their worst. These words of wisdom have helped me through the years as I have experienced the highs and lows of marriage.

After I presented Angela with the ring, she told me that I needed to get everything out of my system before marriage. So, since I had no other vices except girls and now had her permission, I attempted to oblige her.

However, after doing her investigative research, she did find out about another young lady I had shown interest in and decided to break off our engagement. She cut me off, gave me back my ring, went back to school, and found another boyfriend. This totally broke my heart. It devastated me to the point that I went into a state of depression. Angela would not return any of my phone calls. Love is an amazing thing. The old saying goes, "*You never miss your water until your well runs dry."* Truly my well had run very dry.

Through that experience I learned that men and women receive intimacy and love in two different ways. Women take intimacy very seriously; it seems to consume them emotionally and rocks their world when infidelity takes place. However, men, who have been born hunters and conquering creatures, do not always intimately connect physical relationships to love and commitment. Unfortunately, this has been the way men have been taught and are the examples that have been set before us many times.

I could not believe Angela would do this to me. After all, she told me to get it out of my system. It appeared to me that my world was coming to an end. I was broken and cut off from the woman I loved. I was also embarrassed. How would I explain to everyone why she refused to marry me? I was forced to pick up my broken pieces and move on. Al Green had a song that played continuously on the radio back then: "How Do You Mend a Broken Heart?" I wish I knew the answer to that question because I was truly traumatized and devastated. My heart was broken into many pieces, and I had nowhere to retreat.

This was one of the most traumatic times of my life. I praise God that it did not take her very long to realize that we were meant to be together. A few months later she called my house looking for me. My Aunt Martha answered the phone, but never told me that Angela had called. The breakup had not only affected me, but also my entire family. By the grace of God, we were able to reconnect, and we set a wedding date for December 24, 1977. It was the same day that Angela's mom and dad were married. Her mom encouraged us not to get married on Christmas Eve because the holiday would always take away from our anniversary. Needless to say, we did not take her advice and subsequently our wedding anniversary has always been compromised with family and holiday festivities. Rarely have we been able to celebrate our wedding anniversary separately because of all of the other activities that happen around Christmas Eve. Lesson learned.

Our wedding day was something to behold. On that 24th of December 1977, in the sanctuary of the Westside Baptist Church, Pastor Julius Bonner, Angela's pastor, united us in holy matrimony. The church was decked out with a red and white backdrop. Angela's bridesmaids' dresses were red, and my groomsmen were decked out in red and white tuxedos with red accessories. That Saturday afternoon around 6pm, I stood at the church altar and watched the prettiest sight that I've ever beheld walk down that aisle toward me. As her father, Sidney Marvin Smith, held her arm coming down that aisle, I gazed into her eyes and sang, "You Are So Beautiful to Me." Certainly, she was a beautiful sight for sore eyes to behold. This song has always been one of our favorites because it reminds me of the day I received the most precious gift. That day we crossed the Jordan and picked up a new nugget for a different season of our lives together. We were finally united, and we believed our best days were ahead of us.

I wish I could tell you that our time together has been filled with highs and no lows. But the truth is that marriages don't work, people make them work. As a matter of fact, marriage is hard work. Bringing together two people from two different backgrounds who have been raised differently, experienced life differently, and now are trying to unite for a lifetime, is pretty near impossible. That's why the Bible speaks of a binding cord of 3 strands (Ecclesiastes 4:12): *"A three strand cord is not quickly broken."* The three strands represent God, the groom, and the bride. When you braid these three strands together, it symbolizes the joining of one man, one woman, and God in marriage. Marriage is a Holy Institution, and it is impossible for two unholy people to live in holy matrimony without a holy God holding them together. I am grateful that through trials and tribulations, bad decisions and many mistakes, a God that we both claim as our personal Savior has been our saving grace; holding us together with all of our imperfections as the grace of God abounds.

Even in the business world, there are marriages; they're called partnerships. And you have to be willing to give, take, compromise, communicate, and merge your ideas into one overall vision. At the head of every company is a partnership. Even if there is one CEO, there is always a board of leaders and professionals who decide to work together. Just like in marriage, there must be a decision made to make things work for the greater good.

Since we were married during a winter month, I thought that going to Florida at that time of year would be easy to find hotel accommodations. Therefore, I didn't make a reservation. Little did I know that most people chose to vacation in Florida during the holiday season. We were just two kids who had never really done much traveling, so how were we supposed to know? The night of our wedding we stayed around for a couple of hours for the reception and then left Chattanooga in a monsoon type rain storm, heading toward Cocoa Beach and Key West, Florida. Neither of us had ever been to either one of those locations; however, for me, Cocoa Beach brought to mind the 1965 fantasy sitcom television series, "I Dream of Jeannie" that I often watched as a kid. Jeannie was a beautiful blonde woman played by actress Barbara Eden, who lived inside a bottle. She falls in love with an astronaut, played by actor Larry Hagman. The setting of the show was Cape Canaveral, located in Cocoa Beach, Florida. I always thought Cocoa Beach sounded romantic and would be a neat place for our fantasy to begin. After all, I had seen Genie fall in love in this place so what better place to take the love of my life on our honeymoon. Needless to say, our honeymoon wasn't all that great. First of all, it was raining so hard the night we left Chattanooga that we ended up driving about 60 miles outside of Chattanooga to Calhoun, Georgia, then pulling off the highway to get a motel room for the night. It was raining so hard that our honeymoon theme song should have been, "A Rainy Night in Georgia." It seemed like it was "raining all over the world."

Angela and I were both so exhausted from the wedding and all of the activities leading up to it, that when our heads hit the pillows, we both went right off to sleep. That was fine because I now had the woman I had been waiting for so long, we had an exciting honeymoon planned, and we had each other forever. The next day we got up and took off toward Cocoa Beach. After we pulled off, Angela realized that we had left a pair of her shoes back at the motel. She immediately encouraged me to go back and get them. I hated those brown, flat, square-toed, duck-looking shoes. I thought they were the ugliest shoes I had ever seen! I told her that I would not go back for them, but I would buy her some new shoes; however, that did not go over well, and consequently, we embarked upon our first argument as a married couple. We were not one day into what I had hoped would be a joyful rest of our lives, and some ugly shoes had shattered my world. We drove all day and night and finally checked into a hotel on Cocoa Beach around 1:00 a.m. Monday. As soon as we got in bed, it felt like something was crawling on us. When we turned on the lights, we saw bed bugs all over the bed. We were so outdone that we quickly packed up all our clothes, threw them in the car in the middle of the night, and headed towards Key West.

Later the next day, we pulled into Miami. When we arrived, we could not find any rooms vacant on Miami Beach. Disappointed and frustrated, we decided to head on toward Key West, confident in knowing that when we arrived, we would be able to get a room and enjoy the Florida sunshine and beautiful beaches. Wrong again! After taking off for Key West, the traffic was so thick and moving at such a slow pace, it ended up taking us 8 hours in the baking hot sun to travel from Miami Beach to Key West, over what is known as the Overseas Highway. This highway takes you to the southernmost part of the Keys. After eight long grueling hours, we arrived in Key West and guess what? You got it; there were NO rooms available. Our honeymoon started like the story of Mary and Joseph when Jesus was to be born; everywhere they went, there was no room in the inn. Tired, frustrated, and out done, we made a U-turn. We decided to head back across the long, hot highway, toward Daytona, Florida to spend the remainder of our honeymoon week.

After returning home to Chattanooga from our disappointing honeymoon, we went to my parents' home to start our life together. We had applied for a new apartment complex that was expected to be finished a month ahead of our wedding; however, they ran into some delays and did not meet the completion deadline, so we ended up moving in with my parents while waiting for the completion of the new complex.

Moving in with our parents was not the ideal situation. I had waited some ten years to get with the love of my life and have her privately for myself to get to know her more intimately. Needless to say, it was very uncomfortable knowing that the paper thin walls and the squeaky bed that knocked against the upstairs bedroom wall reported our every movement. Certainly, this was not the ideal way to start our lives together, but I thank God for Angela who has always been my ride or die partner. She never complained about our living conditions and fit right in with my family, who literally adored her. My mom and my sister formed a relationship with her that made me jealous. After waiting so long to be with the love of my life, I still felt left out and sometimes even alone. My parents received Angela as their proud "daughter-in-love," and *they* all lived happily ever after!

It's important that the people on your team have a sort of respect and family-like admiration for one another. No matter what level you are working on, treating each other like strangers is never a good recipe for unified success. What my mother, sister, and wife did was the epitome of what teams must do. Spend time together, learn from one another, and be willing to help each other carry the load – when possible and necessary.

Four or five weeks later, after returning from our honeymoon, Angela started to experience morning sickness. We both went to the health clinic to have her checked out. Lo and behold, after her tests were completed, the doctor reported that we were expecting our first child. I did not know how to feel. We had waited so long to become one and I wanted to have everything in place for her to make our life comfortable before we started raising a family. We were only a few weeks into our marriage, still living with my parents, and now I'm being told that we are about to add another person to our family. What am I to do? I am only a child myself trying to maneuver a new season of adulthood and responsibility. I knew that being a husband and a father were positions of responsibility, leadership, and protection. I had observed those things in my father. Still, I didn't quite know how to feel about this news. I think my lack of enthusiasm did not sit well with Angela. I truly was excited, but up until now, nothing in our marriage had worked out according to my plan. Things were moving much too fast and everything I visualized had not come to pass. Number one, after waiting so long to be with my wife, there were too many people around.

My mother was not too excited about the news either. I believe she was thinking that people were going to believe that Angela was already pregnant when we got married. Some people did say it. However, we knew the truth and refused to let the opinions of others deter us. As the pregnancy moved forward, Mom, Angela, and my sister developed a deeper bond and friendship as they enthusiastically shopped and prepared for our first child and my parents' first grandbaby. Several months later, our apartment was completed, and I was so ready to be alone with my wife before the next chapter of our lives' journey began.

Adulthood

Adulthood is about responsibility. My definition of responsibility is "having the ability to properly respond in every situation." Responding to your own self as you are growing is one thing, but being responsible for a wife and now a child-to-be is a totally different scenario. I was about to cross over and dive head first into another season of life. With no roadmap or handbook, I had to rely on what I knew and what I had picked up from the two wonderful people who raised me. I was blessed to have a caring and responsible mother and father who made sure their children came first. As a child I never had to wonder if there would be food on the table, lights on, or whether the water would be cut off. I always knew that my father would do whatever was legally necessary to make sure his wife and children had everything we needed. Now, that mantle was about to fall squarely on me. With my new bride in tow and the announcement of my first child, it was now time for me to step up to the plate.

In your professional life, stepping up to the plate is non-negotiable. If you have several tasks or assignments that you've been entrusted with, you must remember that you are well able to manage them all. However, a good leader knows how to breathe, delegate, and keep the main thing the main thing.

Thinking back on the journey of my firstborn, after the initial shock wore off, I really became excited about the possibility of becoming a father. I had always dreamed the American dream of having a wife, a house with a white picket fence, and an awesome family. It had been my desire to have two sons and a daughter to complete my ideal family unit.

Now, after Angela presented the news that I was going to be a father, I began to speculate what it would be like. For the next month, Angela continued to experience morning sickness and it seemed like each evening, she and her newfound girlfriends went shopping with excitement and enthusiasm for the new baby.

On September 4, 1978, I woke up with plans to drive my brother, Michael, and my brother-in-law, Sidney Marvin Smith Jr., back to school in Nashville Tennessee. Both had enrolled at Tennessee State University and classes were about to start. After a long hot summer, it was my responsibility to make sure they got back to campus. That morning, Angela mentioned to me that she thought she was having labor pains; however, I assured her that they were false labor pains. I thought it was too early for delivery. I dropped her off at my parent's house and headed off to Nashville. On my way back to Chattanooga that afternoon, I received a call informing me that Angela was now in the delivery room. I hurriedly sped back toward home and headed straight to East Ridge Hospital.

Angela was already on the delivery table when I arrived. They rushed me into my hospital fatigues and led me into the room where she was now ready to deliver. I was both nervous and excited to know that I was about to become a father, and grateful that I had made it back in time to witness the birth of my first child, a son. It was my desire to name him something else; however, Angela was determined to name him after me. I had lived all of my life defending my name and did not want to burden any other human being with the same challenge. However, Angela insisted that our son be named Ternae Tsargaris Jordan, Jr. Like my parents, who dedicated me back to God, we presented our bundle of joy back to God, praying for his covering and protection.

After "TJ" was born, I was in my second year of teaching high school. It was no secret that within the three and a half years since I had finished high school and faced the challenge of returning to my own alma mater as a teacher, kids were not the same. One day in class, a young man who I knew well – from the neighborhood – challenged me. Yes, even when you are serving in any leadership capacity, there will always be someone attempting to challenge you and pull you backwards.

I grew up with this kid and his family and had even encountered him and his family in church. This kid stood up in the middle of class and politely invited me to plant my lips on his hind side! I immediately knew I was being tested and tried by this group of 18 year olds and also knew that if I failed the test, I was doomed. I totally blanked out. When I snapped out of it and my consciousness returned, I realized I had snatched this kid up, drug him out into the hall, and had him pinned up against the metal lockers. As I snatched him up and reared back to punch him in the face, it occurred to me that I could not treat someone's kid like this. I immediately released him from the lockers and marched him down to the principal's office. After pleading my case with the principal, he suspended the kid for one day. The very next day, the kid was back in my class. That was the moment I realized that if I didn't want to spend the rest of my life in prison for the murder of someone's child, I had better find another job. After all, things were going relatively well, but I was totally dissatisfied in my own personal life. In the back of my mind, I was still struggling with an inner battle of what my life's purpose truly was.

There was indeed a call on my life to preach the gospel, but I wanted no part of it. I had observed my father and how people reacted to him when he entered a room. I was a fun-loving, people loving, kind of guy. I did not want the stigma of entering a room and having people change their behavior when they saw me. There was this inner struggle that I continued to contend with; however, in the back of my mind, I knew that I would never find any real peace until I accepted the call that had been placed on my life to preach the Gospel of Jesus Christ. Still, I continued to rebel.

When you are a leader, called for a specific purpose and a certain set of people, you can only fight it for so long. The more you attempt to rebel against destiny, the harder your fight will become. Additionally, more people are missing out because you refuse to show up to the seat that only you are qualified to fill.

Rather than answer the call on my life, I subsequently accepted a job with Johnson & Johnson in their personal products division. I became a sales representative in Chattanooga and the surrounding area. My territory consisted of Chattanooga, Nashville, and the Huntsville, Alabama areas. Sales were my background. Remember, I majored in marketing in college and taught it at the high school level. I believed I could sell anything. I quickly was promoted to territory manager after only eight months.

One Thursday evening, I received a call from my district manager, Dave Parks, who told me he was flying in from Indianapolis the next day to take me to dinner. I immediately thought, *"What did I do wrong?"* I just knew he was flying in to reprimand me for something. The next day I picked him up at the airport and we went to dinner. As I sat there, nervously wondering when the hammer would drop on me and end my sales career, he looked across the table and said, *"Ternae, we don't hire sales people, we hire managers. You have done such an awesome job these past eight months that I would like to promote you to territory manager."* As I sat there, I could not believe my ears. How is it that after only eight months on the job, I was promoted to territory manager? He asked me, *"Do you accept it?"* I was baffled as I internally questioned, *"You're offering me a job you want me to accept on the spot and I haven't even had time to talk to Angela or make any plans?"* I told him that I would speak to Angela about it. He encouraged me to do so then reached across the table and handed me an airline ticket. He said, *"Talk to Angela over the weekend and be on this flight to Evansville, Indiana first thing Monday morning."* I was shocked, excited, and nervous. Beyond being on a few trips to Chicago in high school and college, I had never been across the Mason-Dixon line. Now, I was being asked to move to another location and start a new season in my life. Not just that, but I was being asked to move my little family to a new place, a new territory, and start life afresh.

After dinner I took him to the hotel where he was staying then I rushed home to break the news to Angela. She was both excited and nervous about having to make a move so fast. After a brief conversation, we both agreed that I should take the challenge. So, first thing that Monday morning, I was on a flight headed to a new place for a new challenge in a new season in my life.

That Monday morning as I boarded the plane in Chattanooga, I was excited, yet apprehensive. The flight was smooth and within an hour and 30 minutes, the pilot came on the intercom and stated that we were about to land in Evansville, Indiana. Looking out of the window, as far as I could see, were nothing but corn fields and farmland. As we descended from the sky with turbulence rocking our small plane, I thought, *"This has to be one of the most rural places I have ever seen."* As a child, my family spent much time in northern Alabama, looking at cotton fields and even enjoying some country living. But this place looked like the most barren desolate land I had ever seen. As I disembarked, it appeared that I had gone back in time. I proceeded to call a cab to head toward the Executive Inn, the hotel where a room had been reserved for me by the company. Later, I picked up a company car that had been reserved as one of the perks of being a territory manager. I then returned to the hotel to get a good night's sleep. The next day I began to tour the new land I had been led to. The only real assurance I had as I experienced this new place was the assurance that the Lord was with me. I imagined my life being like when God spoke to Joshua: *"Ternae, as I was with Moses so shall I be with you."* I also heard God saying to me, *"As I was with Melvin, so shall I be with you."* It was with that confidence that I started the new season.

New seasons often come when we least expect it, and they often place us in arenas we know not of. This area was probably not something I would have chosen for myself, but it was exactly what was needed. Sometimes, leaders are called to places that look unproductive. But that's just it – as a leader, you have to go where lack appears because you are the one who will change the trajectory of the present.

For two weeks, I drove through my new territory looking for an apartment to bring my wife and newborn son to. I ran across a new apartment complex called the Normandy

Place Apartments. I quickly returned to Chattanooga and packed up my wife and kid to start our new life in Indiana.

It was a very lonely time in life. I traveled a lot in some very rural areas where people of color were not present or allowed. Angela was a trooper through it all, as she remained in our new home with our newborn son. The job left the two of them alone constantly. We had no friends and no connection or ties to this new place. After about two years, I began to feel restless. I encountered many racial situations in those rural towns. One day, as I came out of a store, there were two older white gentlemen in overalls who were standing in the doorway. I kindly spoke, but they never uttered a word. I went in and performed my tasks.

Afterwards, I returned to my car and jumped on Interstate Highway 64, heading back to my wife and son. I was driving at around 65 miles an hour when my front tire began to shake drastically. When I pulled over and got out to check to see what the problem was, I found that all four lugs had been removed from the tires. I could have been killed. I immediately called my company and asked if they would transfer me to a more urban place where people of color worked. They quickly told me they did not move people until they were ready. I had a wife and young child. I could not take the chance of someone hurting me, or better yet, me having to hurt someone to protect my family. I made up my mind that if they didn't move me, I would resign and head back to Chattanooga. I knew that I had left a good name and reputation in Chattanooga and finding a job would not be a problem. I called my cousin and my uncle, loaded up a moving truck, and moved my family back to my hometown.

A real leader knows when to cut their losses. Yes, you can give your all and do everything that you are supposed to do. Yet, there must be a level of wisdom within that nudges you to know when the brook has run dry. And while I'm certain that greater things could have been done in this area, the leader role in me for my family took over and showed me that it was time to bow out gracefully.

Leaders should never be afraid to do the same. Continuing down a path, just to prove a point - even if valid - could be detrimental to the people you are assigned to, as well as yourself.

I immediately got a job back home with the Chattanooga public school system as the director of the Youth Employment training program where I trained students in the mornings on how to get and keep a job. I also coordinated their job placements in the afternoons. I enjoyed my new position and was able to help a lot of kids find employment.

DeJuan's Birth

Upon our return to Chattanooga, we reunited with our family and friends. We also welcomed a new addition to our family. On March 14, 1981, God gave us a wonderful gift in the person of a daughter, DeJuan Shunyal Jordan. I had prayed that the Lord would give us a girl child to go along with our son and dreamed she would be someone who would reflect the beauty and grace of my Angela Faye.

DeJuan's entrance into the world became another milestone in my life, as I crossed the Jordan again into parenthood for the second time. Raising children, especially sons, is difficult. But now, I had a girl child, one who would need to be graceful enough to be a lady, yet strong enough to stand on her own and not have to depend on anyone or another male to make her who she is. I remember the first time I laid eyes on her. She had beautiful sparkling eyes that took my breath away. As she grew, Angela loved to place beautiful bows on her little ponytail.

We never know what we need, as a leader, until it shows up and highlights gaps that only it can fill. When the right person, opportunity, or information comes along, pay attention to how it can positively change you. Yes, change is good and must be appreciated – especially when it's ordained.

Chapter 7 Building Blocks

1. While change might be unexpected and uncomfortable, never let anyone feel comfortable with disregarding or disrespecting you. There is a time and place for formalities, and boundaries must be set. But simple conversations can bring about another level of understanding.

2. No matter where you are destined to go, there will always be provision and space for you. While the unknown is irritable to you because it leaves you

with no control, recognize that there is always something specifically for you. You need only embrace it.

3. Leaders never stay in a dry, unwelcoming place *just* to say that they've remained. There must be fruit where you are. If there is no fruit and all efforts have been exhausted, know when to bow out gracefully. Not only does a leader know when to stick and stay, but when to release and relocate.

CROSSING JORDAN

DR. TERNAE JORDAN, SR.

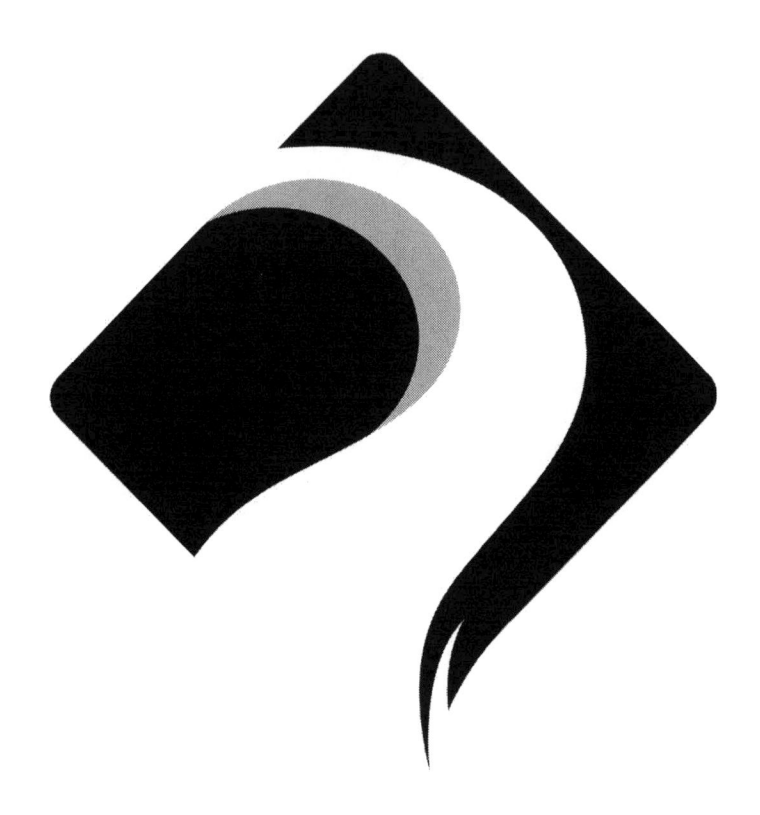

CHAPTER 8

Call into Ministry: The Story

Back in Chattanooga, I quickly returned to my duties at Mount Canaan Baptist Church. I was ordained a deacon, sang in the choir, directed the choir, and served as the head of the Layman's group, our men's ministry. I was truly beginning to feel the tug on my heart that had been placed in me as a child to preach the gospel. Yet, I refused. One night after emceeing a gospel concert, Angela and I were leaving when a singer walked up to me and tapped me on the shoulder. He asked if my name was Ternae Jordan. I thought it was a joke; after all, I had been singing and pumping the program up all evening. Of course, he knew what my name was. He proceeded to tell me that the Lord had told him that I had been called to preach. This was the last thing I wanted to hear. As I grabbed a pregnant Angela by the hand and literally dragged her down the steps, he proceeded to follow us and again said to me, *"Jordan don't do like I did when the Lord was trying to get me to surrender to Him. I was in a car on a lonely dark Mississippi Highway. Don't make Him get your attention in a tragedy."*

What he said rang a bell with me. I remember hearing the story of my father when he was running from ministry. He often told me how he had been in the hospital sick enough to die, but the doctors could not find anything wrong with him. After struggling in pain, he finally turned his face to the wall one night, much like Hezekiah had done, and told God that he would surrender to the call. The next morning, he got up, put on his clothes, and left the hospital never to return again.

At this point, I am now frightened by the singer's words. I had been dealing with this uneasy feeling for so long. I'd always known it was my destiny to preach the gospel, but I was also aware that once I crossed that line, there was no turning back. After this encounter, I knew I had no choice but to surrender to the call that God placed on my life at six years old. Now was the time! I immediately went into prayer. Then early one morning, when I could not rest, I hesitantly picked up the phone and called my dad. It was 6am when he groggily picked up the phone and without hesitation I blurted out, I need to talk to you." I needed to talk to the only person whom I trusted to understand. A leader always needs another leader, a mentor, and wise counsel. He was that for me. I don't know what I needed him to say. He asked if I wanted to come to his house or meet him at his office. I chose the office. I got dressed, snuck out of the house, and nervously rolled to 2800

CROSSING JORDAN

North Chamberlain Avenue, the location of Mount Canaan Baptist Church. When Dad pulled up, we went inside and I immediately blurted out, *"Daddy, I think I have been called to preach."* The words that came from his mouth were definitely not the words I wanted to hear: *"Ternae, I'm not surprised."* He told me that I needed to go spend time in prayer. I responded, *"I don't want to pray. I'm not trying to get closer to God, I'm trying to get away from him."* After talking for a while, he prayed with me. I left his office that morning knowing my life would never be the same. I had now crossed over Jordan again into a new season from which I could never return.

I preached my first sermon in July 1983 to a packed house. People came from all over to witness my first public sermon. It was standing room only; over 500 people were turned away because there was no space in the building. Many people had been expecting this for years. All I heard since my public announcement was "I told you so." Isn't it funny how those who know you are a leader, know you are called to lead, will always remind you that you're running from leading?

Leaving my dad's office, we had to push our way through the crowd to get to the pulpit and there was, as far as I could see, a sea of people waiting anxiously for what they had been waiting to hear for almost 20 years. I was now 26 years old, had been running from this call all my life, and the time had finally arrived. My sermon title that night was, "You Can Run, But You Cannot Hide." It was the story of Jonah who refused to go to Nineveh to declare God's word to the people. I, like Jonah, had refused for so long and found myself in an emotional and traumatic place inside the belly of a large fish that would only release me after I surrendered. This served as an emotional release for me. I was finally letting go of a personal struggle that had entrapped me since childhood. I now felt free, like the weight of the world had been lifted off my shoulders.

After that initial sermon, I never returned to Mount Canaan because I was preaching two or three times every Sunday. That year, I preached 13 revivals in the city of Chattanooga, which was unheard of for a young preacher. My ministry took off so fast that it was almost blinding to me. Eight months after my first sermon, there were five churches looking for a pastor that offered me their pulpit. Of those five, I had my own pecking order. I told the Lord I wanted to go where He wanted me to go; however, there was one of the churches I did not want to pastor. Yet, as only God could do, that is the church that He chose for me to start my new season of pastoring.

When you are called to lead a specific group of people or complete a definite assignment, the ramifications around it aren't usually your favorite. Success does not happen by you always getting what you want. Instead, it happens when you do what's necessary to manifest the outcome needed – that can ultimately only come through you. Leaders don't always get to pick and choose how they lead; they simply must show up to lead and let things align in time.

Bethlehem Baptist Church was located in North Chattanooga, across the river. It was located in the Hill City community, a historical Black community that was started during slavery. It had a history of not following and getting rid of pastors down through their 100 year history.

It had been known as the "pastor incubator" because many pastors they fired went on to have successful ministries in other places.

Bethlehem had a horrible reputation, but after being assured that this was the place that the Lord wanted for me and having His assurance that He would be with me, I accepted the challenge and embarked upon five of the most challenging years of my ministerial journey. I thought with God on my side and my enthusiastic personality, God and I would be able to handle anything, but Bethlehem quickly taught me that my personality did not mean a thing. If I was going to survive there, it was going to be only by the grace of God.

It was at Bethlehem that I truly learned how to pray and trust God in all kinds of situations. It was a family church that had been controlled by families and did not allow pastors to come in and lead. I always felt that I was a born leader, and I would not allow the sheep to lead me. I grew up watching my dad lead. He taught me that God calls pastors to shepherd the sheep, not for the sheep to lead the shepherd. At all times, a leader has to be cognizant of their role and their place. It doesn't matter who wants to do what you do; they will never be able to - at least not 100% effectively.

There was one lady who had much influence in the community and in the church. She was the biggest giver, did things for people in the community, and then held it over their heads to get them to follow her. It did not take long for me to realize that she and I were on a collision course.

I preached and the church grew. The first year, we took in approximately 60 people who didn't normally drive across the river to North Chattanooga. The people knew me and wanted to serve under my leadership, so they flocked to the church. Many souls were added to the church, and we made many improvements to the building, which needed them after 100 years. I kept the congregation pretty busy. Needless to say, some in the community did not take a liking to new people treading on their territory and had no problem letting them know. Sadly, not everyone will always welcome the change that they need. They'll also not be willing to embrace the sent ones. Even so, real leaders and real transformation agents don't allow the side chatter to keep them from hearing the sound of growth.

In my second year as pastor, I learned a powerful lesson. When you don't give people something to do, they will turn their attention and focus it on you. That second year, the wolves were let loose. We would have great service on Sunday. The Lord would bless us. I would preach a powerful message and leave church feeling excited and energetic. But by the time I returned to the community on Wednesday for Bible study, the "phone committee" would have already been gossiping and lying about all kinds of untrue scenarios. When leaders don't task the team with productive assignments, they will make up things to do that cause chaos. The community had communication much like the Underground Railroad. Someone would light a flame and set the whole community on fire, which made it difficult to sustain a vibrant, growing church. It didn't take me long to realize that it was my name that hung on the pastor's office door, but the real pastor of Bethlehem was the one with the influence and the power to rid the church of its previous pastor. She was now on the warpath to get rid of me. She made my life pure hell. Some people want to lead so badly, they can't comprehend that leading begins with following and serving.

One communion Sunday, two and a half years in, I was standing to deliver my prepared message and observed people in the congregation yawning, looking at their watches, and turning to look at the clock on the back wall. In the middle of the message, a voice inside my head spoke to me and said, "This is it." I politely closed the message, came down out of the pulpit, stood behind the communion table, and uttered these words: *"I now know how Jesus must have felt in the Upper Room at the Last Supper with his disciples because this is our last supper together."* Half of the church roared and shouted for joy, while the other half broke down in tears. Enough was enough. I did not have to take the negativity being dished out. I left Bethlehem Baptist Church that day. I felt as if the world had been lifted off my shoulders, yet in my spirit I knew that the voice in my head was not the voice of God. I had made the decision to walk away from God's people and I knew He was not pleased. Pastoring God's people can be hard. I knew this before I accepted the call, which is why I ran for so long. Realizing that I had made a major mistake, I prayed that God would give me a way to reconcile the decision that I had made against Him.

On Tuesday of that same week, two carloads of young people drove up to my house. They had petitions that were signed by 80 church members. I tried to act tough, but I knew this was God's way of opening the door for me to reconcile with Him and His people. I told the young people that we could meet on Tuesday evening, but there were things that had to change. That Tuesday evening the church was full. I stood up, and with a strong voice declared that if I were to return as their pastor, there would need to be changes and better cooperation from the people. They agreed they would do better if I returned and so I returned as their pastor. They were right. They were indeed better for two weeks, then the same activities and personalities returned. I learned, much like Moses did each time he went to God and told the Lord about His stiff-necked people: *"I'm going to leave them in your hands."* I learned the valuable lesson that my job is not to make people do right. That's God's job. My job is to preach, teach, and tell them what the Word says. And that certainly freed me of some impossible responsibilities.

As you take on supervisory roles or any roles where you are assigned to people, you can only do what YOU can do. Even when you have the greatest intent and deliver with compassion, some will simply reject you. A mature leader will remember that it's their job to set the table, but it's not their job to force feed anyone. When they're hungry, they'll eat. If they don't eat, they'll starve. Never allow the art of leadership to become forceful and domineering. When you get to that point, you've already lost the battle.

Bethlehem was only able to pay me $150 a week, which was impossible to raise a family on and provide the necessities they needed. While working for the school system, I met Willie Bob Johnson, a young man who became a lifelong friend to me. Willie Bob worked for the Boys Club and had hired a number of my students for work-study jobs. He and I became remarkably close. Willie Bob decided to start his own business and he named it KBL Enterprises. "K" after his daughter, Keisha; "B" after his son, Brian; and "L" after his wife, Lillie. Because of my teaching experience and work with young people, Willie Bob asked if I would join his company and become his executive director of teaching and training. Between KBL and Bethlehem, I was able to make a decent salary in order to provide for my family.

Willie Bob and I did great things together. The company grew and we even won the minority business award for the state of Tennessee. We were doing well as two young African American men making an impact in the city. As always, when young African American males are doing well, the system always finds a way to negate our success. We were at the top of our game when the City of Chattanooga decided to discontinue funding us. They took a $120,000 contract from us and gave another $600,000 contract to an organization that did not even touch the kids and communities who needed it the most. After that, Willie Bob made the decision to move back to Omaha, Nebraska where he and his family had originated. That summer, Willie Bob and I drove back and forth to Omaha in order to keep the business going. As Willie Bob was making his decision to return home, I was wondering what I would do to provide for my family. I tried everything. I even sold water filters, which I could not move. I had plenty of them left for the next phase of my life.

On April 2, 1988, my youngest son, JaMichael Jordan, was born into the Jordan. It was my third time around, but again it was one of the happiest days of my life, as I stood gazing at the content of the hospital's baby crib, labeled "Jordan 5086." JaMicheal Darnell Jordan had made his arrival into the world. Here lying before me was my third child and second son. However, we were disappointed to find out that during delivery, he had been born with facial palsy. It had been a difficult delivery due to the negligence of the nurse attendant, failing to completely empty Angela's bladder, which caused a ripple effect of issues. At birth, my baby boy's heart rate began to drop rapidly. In the haste of that moment, forceps were improperly used, which resulted in his being born with facial palsy. As I stood by that crib numbered "5086 Jordan," despite the damage, nothing could take away the pride I felt. As I lifted him up, I knew I was looking at another part of me, a man-child, and the next branch of my Jordan Legacy. I knew that just like my other two blessings, he would one day impact the world for the greater good and make it a better place because of this Jordan heritage.

As a result of the damage to JaMichael's face, he could not open his right eye; however, as I held that small piece of humanity in my hand, I declared, "JaMichael Darnell Jordan, open your eyes." Words cannot express the emotions I felt as he struggled but finally was able to open his left eye. I was overwhelmed with joy because I knew this bundle of joy was destined for greatness. Leaders know when and how to use the power of their words. If you enter a space that is not conducive for progression, speak to it. Success is in the atmosphere, and it always responds to confident faith.

Facial palsy is the paralysis or loss of facial movement, caused by damaged nerves, which causes the muscles to droop and weaken. There are many causes for facial paralysis; however, in this case, the doctor had damaged him by applying too much pressure and squeezing too hard with the forceps during a hurried delivery. The facial paralysis he suffered made it difficult for him to eat or to nurse. On the day Angela left the hospital, we had to leave our baby boy behind. At home, Angela rested. Five days later, I went to the hospital with Iciephine and my mother to bring him home, still struggling with palsy. Angela was so excited to finally get her baby home where he belonged. Six weeks later, we were preparing to take him for his six-week check-up. The night before his appointment, Angela was getting him ready for bed, as we stood over him, praying and asking God to heal and bless him. The next morning, as she was preparing him for his doctor's visit, I heard this loud scream from our bedroom, "Ternae, Ternae, his palsy is gone." Hallelujah. God had heard our cry again and answered our prayers, as He would continue to do as we continued along this journey of crossing Jordan.

Again, I say, leaders have undeniable faith and the ability to decree a thing, establishing it. When was the last time that you audibly spoke what you needed to see in your home, office, or organization? When was the last time you spoke over that written vision, commanding it to be productive and create increase? The leader in you must recognize the language of faith and ingenuity.

Also, at this time I had grown weary of Bethlehem and felt

like the Lord was calling me elsewhere, but doors would never open. I began putting in resumes at different churches everywhere in the surrounding areas. Several churches promised me that I would be their next pastor. One such church, Thankful Baptist Church in Rome, Georgia, went as far as to take a church vote, but when it was taken, certain members voted for one of their relatives. I was told that if they did not hire the relative, it would tear up the church, so they passed on me. I was extremely disappointed and devastated, but there was another church. Damascus Baptist Church in Cartersville, Georgia was interested in me becoming their next pastor. They told me that if Thankful Baptist did not call me, they would hire me as their pastor. I went back to preach and meet with them. They were to have a business meeting on the following Wednesday night and promised to call me after the meeting to let me know that I had been selected. This sounded like a sure thing to me. When Wednesday came, no call. The next Wednesday came, still no call. I was getting very restless, but I was too proud to call them to see what had transpired. Then one Sunday morning, I was lying in bed and dreading getting up to go to Bethlehem. All of my faithful members had long been run off. Some would come by and tell me how much they loved me and liked my preaching, but they could not stay because of all of the hostility in the church. I did not feel comfortable asking them to stay because I too wanted to leave.

I began to sense an urge that God was preparing me for another assignment. Willie Bob had moved back to Omaha. He, Lillie, and their family were a major part of our success. I was his pastor and boss on Sunday, and he was my boss during the week. It felt like part of my soul had been ripped away. I wished them the best and looked forward to what was next in my life. It definitely hurts when you lose a valued asset to the team, but the show must go on.

I was disappointed that I had not heard from Damascus Baptist Church, but that Sunday morning while lying in bed, the telephone rang. The voice on the other end said, *"Pastor Jordan, this is Deacon Whitfield from Damascus Baptist Church in Cartersville, Georgia. I'm calling to let you know that we decided we cannot afford a pastor of your caliber."* What? Was this supposed to be a compliment? I'm willing to drive 90 miles one way, 180 miles round trip weekly. I'm almost willing to pay you to allow me to be your pastor and you have the nerve to say you cannot afford a pastor of my caliber. Once again, I was devastated. I got up to go to the bathroom. I locked the door because I did not want to disturb Angela or have her come into the bathroom and find me sobbing. I looked in the mirror and tears began to fall. I knew I had been disappointed, but I also knew that I was in the will of God. At that moment I dried my eyes, stared into the mirror, and said, *"God, it is obvious that you did not want me in either of those places, so here's what I'm going to do. I'm going to dry my eyes, shower, then go over here where you planted me, and I am going to give you 110% of me until you say I'm done."*

I did exactly that and when I got to the church, two elderly ladies who had been instrumental in clearing out the church, were leading devotion. One was singing and the other was praying. I took a seat on the front pew, devastated and angry at where I was at that moment. When I heard the phone ringing in my office, I got up and went out to answer the phone. When I picked up the phone, the voice on the other end began to talk without breathing for what seemed like 10 minutes. This voice said, *"This is Deacon Eddie Nelson from the Greater Progressive Baptist Church in Fort Wayne, Indiana, and we're looking for a pastor. We want to know if you would be willing to come up and preach for us."* I stood there in awe. It had not been an hour since I looked in the mirror and promised God that I would be faithful and give him 110% of me and now, less than an hour later, my phone is ringing. I stood there frozen. I tried to speak, but my words would not come. I finally uttered, *"Yes, I'm willing to come."* He asked if I could come next week, and I said "no" because that was Christmas Day. He then asked if I could come the following week, and I again said "no" because that's New Year's. He then asked, *"How about the second Sunday in January?"* We confirmed the date, I hung up, and immediately called Angela who was at home with our youngest child, JaMichael. I said, *"Angela we're moving."* She asked, *"Moving where?"* When I told her we were moving to Fort Wayne, she asked *"Where is that?"* I told her it was somewhere in Texas. I knew at that very moment that God had finally heard my cry and was releasing me from this assignment for a new season in my life that would propel me into a new hemisphere of ministry. I went back to Sunday school on a cloud. I don't remember what happened the rest of that day, but I do know that I learned another valuable lesson. So many times, we're waiting for God to bless us and open doors for us, but sometimes God is waiting for us to be committed and faithful so He can elevate us to where he wants us to be. The leader in you has to stick and stay. The staying can be lessened when you prove – from the inside out – that you're ready and willing to stick it out.

On January 7, 1989, my wife and youngest son JaMichael, who was 9 months old at the time, embarked on a journey that would change the trajectory of our lives forever. Being a southern boy, I had never traveled that far north in the winter time, so I was unprepared for what I would encounter on my way across the Jordan into this next season. When we left Chattanooga that day, it was sunny and bright with exceptional weather. It wasn't until we arrived in Indianapolis, Indiana that it felt like all hell was breaking loose.

I was thinking that Indianapolis must be the line that separates the south from the north. When we arrived there, frozen ice covered the interstate, some cars were turned upside down, while others slipped off the highway into ditches. The fog was so thick that I could not see anything through the windshield. The best I could do was to look out of my side view mirror to see the slightly visible lines on the road. Angela and JaMichael were sleeping soundly. It was just me and God. I remember praying all the way to Fort Wayne from Indianapolis. My prayer was, *"Lord, you are taking me to new territory. I've had many storms in my life. Please give me the assurance that I need that this next season is going to be a great one for me. I need you to be with me."*

The Lord had given me a sermon to preach, "Does God Ever Send the Storm?" As we passed through Indianapolis, that would be the first of many storms I would experience during my first weekend in Fort Wayne.

We arrived in Fort Wayne around 12:30am on Saturday morning. When we pulled up to the Holiday Inn, the bellhop came out and told us he didn't know what was going on with the weather. The temperature had dropped 50 degrees in the last two hours. I felt if he didn't know what was going on and he lived here, how in the world was I supposed to figure it out? We checked in and went upstairs and called Deacon Eddie Nelson, whom I had promised to call upon our arrival. When he answered the phone, he immediately said, *"I'm coming to pick you up."* No way! I just got here. I had driven all day through the bad weather and had my wife and son, but he would not take no for an answer. He and his brother, Sim Nelson, were two of the leading deacons at Greater Progressive Baptist Church and they picked me up from the hotel. Our short trip led us to 2215 John Street, the location of the Greater Progressive Baptist Church.

We got out in the frigid weather and walked to the front porch of the church. They unlocked the door, and we walked in. They turned on the lights from the back of the church to the front. The aisles were getting longer and longer as the red seats looked like we were in a cathedral. I remember asking God, *"What do you want me to do with all of this?"* I heard him say, *"Just preach."* This was strange. I had not preached here yet, nor met any of the members, but somehow there was this feeling in my spirit that God was getting ready to bust a move. After touring the church, we went back, and got in the car. Then Eddie Nelson turned around to me and asked, *"Do you want this church?"* I responded, *"I don't know, I haven't preached here yet, I haven't met any of the members and I don't know if they want me."* Eddie then said, *"If you want this church, me and my brother can get it for you."* That startled me because what I actually heard was *"If you take this church, me and my brother can take it from you."* They then went on to ask me if I were called to Fort Wayne, would Angela be willing to come? I assured them that Angela was my number one supporter and would be willing to follow me wherever the Lord led us.

After leaving the church, I thought we were on our way back to the hotel. Instead, they made a left turn and headed to the parsonage located at 3515 Autumn Lane. When we got out of the car, we were standing on a dark porch in the frigid weather as Eddie fumbled for the keys to the front door. I'm standing there, afraid that someone will look out of their window and think there are burglars breaking into this empty house. Eddie pulled out his cigarette lighter, finally found the key, and we entered the parsonage that had no lights or heat, the electricity was turned off and with only the light of a cigarette lighter, we toured the house. You could tell they were proud of the parsonage, but I could only think of getting back to my wife and son. It was about 2:30am by then. After the tour, they took me back to the Holiday Inn and told me that someone would pick us up in the morning to take us to the church to meet some of the leaders and the youth department. I laid down that night wondering what God was up to. The next morning, we were picked up and taken to the church where we met some of the youth leaders.

After the meeting, Angela and I went to the mall to walk

around and talk. As we pushed the baby carriage through the mall, I asked Angela the big question: *"If the Lord called me to Fort Wayne, would you be willing to come?"* Just as I already knew, she said, *"Ternae, wherever the Lord is leading you, I will follow."* As we were leaving the mall that day, there were thick dark clouds in the sky. There was no question that a major storm was brewing. We jumped in the car and went and bought pizza. As we pulled back into the Holiday Inn parking lot, the heavens opened up and strong winds began to blow. We took cover as we ran into the hotel and went immediately to our room on the fifth floor. As Angela began to dry the baby off, I went to the window to look out at the storm. The wind was blowing so hard it felt like the window was going to blow back into the room. I looked out at the traffic lights, which the wind had blown above the wires they hung on. Garbage cans were being blown down the street and it became very apparent that a tornado was somewhere close by. I was about to walk away from the window for my own safety when a voice spoke to me and told me what I was preaching that Sunday. The message title given was, *"Does God Ever Send the Storm?"* At that point, I stood and gazed out of that window watching that storm come through because somehow I felt like the storms of my past were blowing away and the trauma of my journey was propelling me to the destiny of my future. I was now Crossing Jordan into a whole new world.

Leaders, look out the window. Most of the time, we see something coming and try to avoid it. An equipped leader, however, will find the silver lining in what appears to be bad and listen for instructions on how to incorporate it for success.

The next morning, January 9, 1989, we woke up early. When I looked out the window for signs of the damage from the previous day's storm, I couldn't believe my eyes. A traumatic storm had come through with high winds and a tornado set down in a suburb of Fort Wayne. Yet, my eyes settled on a blanketing snow that covered the ground. Within 3 days, I had experienced an ice storm, a wind storm with tornadoes, and now a snowstorm. As we got dressed to go to church, my mind was reeling and rocking over what I had experienced these past few days. Within approximately 72 hours, I had seen them all. What kind of message was God speaking to me?

As we gathered at the church, I went into the pastor's study and prayed. When service started, I was led out to the pulpit to a huge nearly empty church. There were about 25 people present. Progressive had always had a great membership; but with each pastor change, the church numbers would rise and fall. As I sat in the middle chair of the pulpit, preparing to preach, I looked out of the front door and there were snowflakes falling as large as my hand. The only thing I could think about was, *"Lord, please let this snow stop because I have to get Angela back to work by Tuesday morning."*

The Lord truly blessed me that day as I shared the sermon He placed upon my heart. Looking back, I'm reminded that many times when God is transitioning and preparing you for your next assignment, the storms of adversity will blow in order to get you to trust Him for your "next level."

After the service, we were invited over to Deacon Sim and Vernell Nelson's house for dinner. As my little family and I entered the doors of the Nelson home, Mother Vernell Nelson screamed in a loud voice, *"Here comes my pastor!"* With those words, I knew that God was now giving me the assurance that I would be the next leader and Pastor of the Greater Progressive Baptist Church.

Mother Nelson had to be one of the sweetest and best cooks that I have ever been around, other than my own mother, Maggie Jordan. She had everything you could possibly think of on that table: collard greens, yams, roast beef, cornbread, pinto beans, beef stew, and so much more. You name it, it was there that day. My little family truly ate until our souls were satisfied. After dinner, we packed up and headed back to our hotel room, driving through the snow covered streets of Fort Wayne. The only thing I could think of was, *"Lord, how in the world will I drive through this snow, so Angela can be back at school on Tuesday?"* It had been a great weekend; however, I knew that in order to get back home I had to drive through adverse conditions, yet I knew that if I could make it though, my future could be bright.

Once back at the hotel, Angela prepared the baby for bed and packed for our return home. I stood in that same window where I had watched the windstorm and cried out to God, *"Lord, if you are saying to me that You have sanctioned this next move, I need You to assure me. For the last three days I have seen nothing but storms. I even preached 'Does God Ever Send the Storms?' as my message."* My sermon text was from the 14th chapter of the book of Exodus; the story of Moses and the children of Israel who were trapped at the Red Sea with no way to cross, but God opened up the sea and made a dry highway through it in order to get them to their land of promise. *"Lord, if this is your way of telling me that this next move is the one you have assigned me, when I wake up in the morning, I need You to give me sunshine so that I can return home knowing that You are still with me."* As I laid down that night, I could not sleep because I knew that what I had asked of God was almost impossible for Fort Wayne for that time of year. I remembered Gideon, who asked God for an impossible sign to prove that He was with him. I needed that same assurance. I don't remember exactly when I dozed off to sleep that night, but I do remember I needed confirmation when I woke up the next morning. I trusted God for his assurance.

The next morning, I woke up early. As I pulled myself out of the bed, my knees were shaking and weak. It was dark in the room. As I headed towards the window to pull back the curtains, I was afraid of what I might see on the other side. I apprehensively opened the curtains to one of the biggest surprises of my life. Slapping me in the face was the bright shining sun. It literally almost knocked me backwards! What had been snow when I laid down the previous night was now melting snow, now water flowing down the streets. I ran back to the bed and shouted, *"Angela, wake up baby, it's time for us to go home!"* We hurriedly packed the car to head back to Chattanooga and I was now sure, even though the church had not yet voted, that I would be the next pastor of the Greater Progressive Baptist Church, located at 2215 John Street, Fort Wayne Indiana. Driving the next eight and a half hours, it seemed, the farther I drove, the brighter the sun and the bluer the skies became. I headed home to prepare myself for the call I knew would come. I began, by faith, to prepare myself to make the transition that would ultimately become the greatest transition and water crossing experience I had ever had in my life.

Once we returned home, the first thing I wanted to do was to locate my father. I wanted to share with him my powerful experience. Before going to preach in Fort Wayne, I asked him if I should go, particularly after hearing all of the negative things about the church. Dad told me not to listen to the negativity of other folks because if the Lord is for you, then He will take care of you and provide for you. Dad had always been my voice of reason. I never had to doubt him. He was truly a man of faith and any time I needed someone to speak into me, he was always there. I didn't have to think about it twice if he said it because I knew that, as his oldest son, he wanted nothing but the best for me. So, if he said it, that settled it. All I needed to do was walk in the advice he had given me. Having a mentor in your life that helps you put the blinders on is a great asset.

Finally came the call. God had sanctioned my transition to this new place and season. Now, the challenge became how in the world I would break the news to Bethlehem. Whenever you move to a new level, it constitutes your leaving something behind. How would they respond? What would they say? As I went into prayer and began to craft my letter of resignation explaining the next move in my life, I agonized over using the right words.

The day that I read the letter, the church was silent. When

I got to the point of mentioning that the Lord was moving me to a new place, pandemonium broke out. To my dismay, half of the people stood up crying, "Oh no!" The other half stood up and clapped. The crowd that seemed to be my most challenging parishioners seemed glad that I was resigning. The lady who had been the most influential negative voice had finally accomplished her goal - yet again. As I shared with the congregation that I would be giving them my 60-day notice, one lady stood up and said, *"If you are going to leave us, why don't you do it today?"* Wow! After five years of blood, sweat, and tears in trying to lead and grow a ministry, this was the thanks I got. I was both relieved and heartbroken. This was the assurance of what I had always thought: "When people can no longer use you, they have no use for you."

Always remember that. Don't lead from that place but be aware of the possibility of that place. I had to lead with integrity, regardless of their responses. And even when their responses - or the lack thereof - hurt me, I had to still be who I was created to be. You cannot afford to stop being you, stop leading, stop serving, stop creating, all because others don't like you. Stand your ground and stand in your place.

That afternoon, we had another service at the church. As I pulled into the parking lot, I noticed another car in my reserved parking spot, so I pulled into another spot and went towards my office. As I opened the door, there - sitting on the desk - were all of my office items and awards packed up in a box. Someone had already packed up my belongings. I tried to remain calm and conduct myself as the Christian I had always tried to exhibit, but with this kind of treatment, I was beginning to feel the release and relief that this chapter of my life was finally behind me. I had already told Progressive that I was going to give Bethlehem 60 days' notice, but Bethlehem chose to relieve me that day. As I closed that chapter, it was a reminder that leading people many times is a thankless job; however, the call to ministry is not about the accolades or even support of the people. The call of God is about the *faithfulness* of his servants to Him. I was reminded that I don't do what I do because of the people; I do what I do because of my faithfulness to God. Why do you do what you do? What is your thriving point? What is your fuel? I realize that the lessons we learn, both good and bad - as we travel life's journeys - are the gems and stones of remembrance that help us to reach our Promised Land and our Destiny. I learned to embrace the challenges. Between the lessons experienced and the stones of wisdom picked up in my Jordan legacy, I would now be able to survive the next leg of my journey.

Thank you, Melvin and Maggie Jordan, for instilling love, hope, and faith within me. You truly prepared me to move deeper into Jordan. And thank you for passing on the baton for the next leg of my journey.

No matter who you are and no matter where you are, take a moment to recognize that you are an amazing asset to the world. And wherever you have been entrusted to serve, remember that every part of your life has already equipped you to do it successfully.

Your Jordan may not look like mine, but it is certainly worth conquering and enjoying all the way through. Now, let's see what happens next…

Chapter 8 Building Blocks

1. Every leader always needs a mentor and someone in whom they can seek wise counsel.

2. Leaders recognize other leaders, no matter what space they might be in. When one identifies you, respect and embrace their affirmation of who you really are, even when you're trying to hide.

3. Just because you are sent "there" doesn't mean everyone "there" will embrace you. Know that you can only lead as much as you are allowed to. Never stop being you, but don't force people to change with you.

4. Losses within the team may come, but don't stay in the funk of the loss. Learn how to highlight the lesson and prepare for the next move.

5. Remember that your words have power. Watch what you establish with your language.

6. The storm may have done damage, but it can also promote destiny. Be aware of what your storm was sent to pluck up and plant.

DR. TERNAE JORDAN, SR.

ABOUT THE AUTHOR

Dr. Ternae T. Jordan, Sr. is a highly respected and accomplished second-generation minister who has dedicated his life to serving God and making a positive impact on the lives of others. Growing up in Chattanooga, Tennessee, Dr. Jordan developed a deep-rooted passion for his faith and a strong commitment to community service.

He obtained a Bachelor of Science degree with a major in Business Education and a minor in Religious Studies from the University of Tennessee. Driven by his desire to expand his knowledge and enhance his leadership skills, he pursued further education at the prestigious Harvard School of Divinity, Leadership Institute, where he received a diploma.

Throughout his 40 years of dedicated service, Dr. Jordan has held significant pastoral positions at notable churches. He began his first pastorate at the Bethlehem Baptist Church in Chattanooga and went on to serve 15 years at the Greater Progressive Baptist Church in Fort Wayne, Indiana. Currently, he serves as the esteemed Pastor of Mt. Canaan Baptist Church in his hometown of Chattanooga, Tennessee.

Beyond his pastoral duties, Dr. Jordan has made a lasting impact on communities through his tireless efforts. In

1992, he founded Stop the Madness, Inc., an anti-violence program aimed at providing cultural, spiritual, and recreational alternatives to at-risk youth. This program has since expanded and evolved into Stop the Madness National, Inc., serving as a beacon of hope and support for young people.

One of Dr. Jordan's notable achievements includes his role as the Program Director of the Value-Based Initiative (VBI) from 1999 to 2004. Funded by the Department of Justice, Office of Community Oriented Policing Services, VBI focused on fostering effective involvement of faith-based communities in making Fort Wayne a safer place. Dr. Jordan played a crucial role in building stronger relations between the minority community and the local police department, ultimately contributing to a safer and more harmonious city.

His exceptional contributions have earned him numerous awards, honors, and recognitions. Dr. Jordan received the degree of Doctor of Divinity honoris causa from Huntington College in Indiana in 2005, in recognition of his outstanding leadership and compassionate service to the community. He has been invited to participate in discussions and panels at national events, including the United States Department of Justice's National Gang Executive Session, where he contributed his expertise on intervention and prevention programs.

Currently, Dr. Jordan serves on several boards and committees, including Purpose Point Community Resource Center, Chattanooga Area Chamber of Commerce, United Way (Executive Board), Stop the

Madness National, Launch CHA, and the Piedmont International University Board of Trustees. He has also played a significant role in important local initiatives such as the National Day of Prayer, Ruth Graham Crusade and Day of Service, and the Pastors Prayer Team for the City of Chattanooga.

Despite his numerous accomplishments, Dr. Jordan remains grounded and dedicated to his faith, family, and community. Alongside his wife, Angela Faye Jordan, he has raised three children (Ternae Jr., DeJuan, and JaMichael) and enjoys spending time with his grandchildren (Deanna, JaMichael Jr., Nason, and Asa). Known for his compassion, sense of humor, and embodiment of the Fruit of the Spirit, Dr. Ternae T. Jordan, Sr. continues to inspire and uplift others through his unwavering commitment to serving God and his community.

Contact Dr. Jordan!

📍 P.O. Box 16326
Chattanooga, TN 37416

📞 423-598-9365

✉ info@drternaejordansr.com

🌐 www.drternaejordansr.com

CROSSING JORDAN

*Volume 1:
Transformational Leadership*

DR. TERNAE JORDAN, SR.

Foreword By: Dr. Delatorro McNeal, II, MS, CSP, CPAE

USA Today & Wall Street Journal Best-Selling Author

Made in the USA
Middletown, DE
01 September 2024